A HORSE'S TALE

BY

BARBARA N. STEWART

Copyright© 2009 by Barbara N. Stewart

Cover photography and all quotes from USERL website copyright© by Jennifer Malpass

Printed in the United States of America

Horses – what little girl hasn't dreamed of owning one! They are the stuff of which dreams are made; they've served man throughout history, fought battles, and plowed fields. They've carried people across continents and opened up new territories. They've been subject to man's superiority since time began, yet man has continually mistreated these magnificent animals. Even today, in 'modern' times, people still do the unthinkable to horses in their care.

This is the story of Sassy – a true story. Since we don't know what life was like for her prior to the time she was rescued, I've taken the liberty of creating that part of the story, but Sassy's rescue and recovery are well documented. Your purchase of this book contributes to the rescue and rehabilitation of countless horses through the United States Equine Rescue League – USERL – but how wonderful it would be to not need such an organization. Thank you for your purchase; countless horses thank you, too.

Barbara Stewart

Chapter One

I'm stretched out on the fresh straw, basking in the sunlight streaming into my stall through the open window. Sleep has been easy here, where I'm safe and secure, full and happy. Such was not always the case, and now that I'm fully recovered from my ordeal, I've decided to share the events of my life.

This is my tale, my story. I'm a miniature mare now named Sassy, you see, and people think I'm really cute because I'm so small, standing a little over 8 hands high. Regular horses tower over me. Big horses don't understand us little guys, and I always wanted to be a big horse, until I met Tank, that is. Tank is my best buddy now, and he's a miniature horse, too, and we spend our days galloping around the pastures as the big horses watch. Life is good now, and Tank is part of that goodness. Goodness should fall upon all living things; that's just the way it should be, but many horses that I've met haven't been blessed with goodness, and that's why I need to tell you my story. Hopefully, when my story is shared, the humans that have horses – or any animal, for that matter – in their care will see that they are treated with respect and dignity and given the things they need to be healthy and happy.

In my short life, I've learned that animals are at the mercy of their caregivers, and it's well-known throughout the horse community that there are many caregivers who fail to take proper care of their horses when it is totally within their power to do so.

I look at Tank, who is sleeping close by. I watch him twitching as he dreams, probably about chasing the frogs down by the pond. His nostrils flare as he breathes a little faster, his short legs mimic running, and I can't help but laugh.

Tank sits up and looks at me. "What's so funny?"

"You!" I answer. "You're so funny when you dream!"

Tank shakes his head, dislodging the pieces of straw trapped there. "I was dreaming?"

"Oh, yes, and you're stubby legs were going like crazy! Too funny, Tank!"

"Well, next time I'll watch and see if you run in your sleep, and then I can laugh at you." Tank stands up and shakes from head to toe. "There, that feels better."

I stand up and do the same. Tiffanygirl spends a lot of time brushing me. It's not that I need that much grooming. I just like being brushed, so I'd much rather be outside rolling in the dirt, which then gives her another reason to groom me.

I observe Tank again. When he arrived here, he was a pudgy little guy, but he's slimmed down quite a bit. He had the craziest hooves I've ever seen; no one had trimmed them for a very long time, and they curved up in the front, making Tank walk on the back of his pasterns, which was very painful for him, but now his hooves are nicely trimmed and he can walk normally. In fact, he can keep up with me when I run! Losing the weight helped him get around, too. Usually the horses that come to this place are nothing but skin and bones, suffering from starvation, but Tank was different; he'd had too much to eat. Running around, now that his hooves are back to normal, has helped him lose the weight, and he's quite fit now. He's told me that he stood around and ate when his hooves and legs hurt, so that's how he got fat.

Anyway, I need to get on with my story. I live at this farm, a rescue farm that saves horses which have been the recipients of ill care or lack of care by their caregivers. All of us here have a story to tell, and maybe someday Dreamer, Cisco, Wrangler, or Rejoice, or any of the others here, may tell you their stories; each is as varied as the horses themselves, and each is pregnant with suffering and mistreatment that no horse should have to endure. It's my understanding that I'm one of the worst cases ever seen and that I'm fortunate to be alive; it's difficult for me to understand what happened to me. I don't ever think I'll understand the 'why'.

But let me get on with it – let me begin my tale.

I was born to a wonderful mother. I still think she's the best mother in the world. She kept me from danger and taught me how to jump high and run like the wind! -- well, as high and as fast as a miniature horse can go! I remember the days of lying in the pastures at the farm where I was born, the sun's rays warming my coat. Mother was always close, quick to protect me from things like snakes and wild dogs which occasionally broke through the fence.

Naturally, Mother was the first to welcome me into the world, and communicating with my mother came before I could stand steadily on my hooves and get my first milk.

Her voice still rings softly in my ears. "Welcome to the world, Little One."

Struggling to get on my spindly legs, I cried, "Help me, Mother! I can't stand up!"

Mother nudged me with her soft muzzle. "I'm sorry, Little One, but that's something you'll have to do all by yourself. All newborn foals must stand on their own without any help."

My legs felt like rubber bands. Despite my best efforts, they bent inward, and every time I tried to hold them steady, I lost my balance and fell into the soft straw.

"Don't worry, you'll be standing in a short time; just don't stop trying." I felt Mother's tongue licking my back, which was still wet for whatever reason, I have no idea.

Using all my strength, I stood again, and this time, I managed to stay upright a while longer, but one move and down I went. Mother laughed! From my position in the straw, I looked up at her and saw a gleam in her eye, and I had to smile in spite of my inadequacies. "Okay, I'll try again."

Before long, I was upright, and this time I didn't fall down! "Yeah! I did it, Mother! I'm standing!" My legs were still swaying sticks under my body, but I was upright.

"Wonderful! Now take a few steps," Mother urged as she nudged me again.

"But I'll fall! I know I will!"

"You'll do just fine, Little One."

Ever so slowly, I lifted one hoof into the air and put it down in front of me; before I knew it, my other legs followed, and I went alongside Mother. "I did it, just like you said, Mother! I did it!" I leaned into Mother's warmth, glad for the extra support.

Just then, I heard a strange sound. "Don't be frightened," Mother said. "It's our caregivers, the ones who take care of me, and now you. They are gentle. They won't harm you. They're excited that you're here."

"Here? Why should they be excited about that?" I asked as I realized that I was hungry and started searching for something to quiet the rumblings in my belly. Don't ask me how I knew where to go – I just did.

Mother stood still as my mouth found her udder tucked up between her hind legs, and I immediately started sucking. The flow of warm milk into my stomach felt good. I stiffened my legs to steady myself.

The door to the paddock opened, and two strange creatures stood in the doorway. They certainly didn't look like Mother. They had four legs, but they stood on only two of them and used the other two to move and hold things. They looked very strange to me.

Mother must have sensed my insecurity. "They are called humans, Little One. They provide this nice place in which you were born."

"Born?" I asked as I stopped nursing and stared at the humans standing in the doorway.

"I'll explain later, much later," Mother replied as she called softly to the humans.

The humans entered the paddock and ran their hands over my mother's body. When one reached for me, I jumped back and promptly landed on my rump. Mother laughed, and I guess the sound the humans made was laughing, too, but it sure was different! I struggled to my feet again, and one of the humans knelt down beside me and wrapped his front leg (which Mother later told me was called an arm) around my neck. He started petting me; it felt good. My fears vanished.

The humans made noises that I couldn't understand, but they petted Mother constantly, and me, too, when I stood still long enough for them to hold me. One of the humans left and returned with a bucket full of oats for Mother – I wanted more milk and set about getting it. Soon, I collapsed on the floor of the paddock and went fast asleep.

And so I entered this world, a world where humans are in control and we animals are at their mercy and subject to them.

* * * * * * * * *

I spent the first day of my life in the paddock with my mother. The humans came and changed the bedding and fed Mother good things to eat; her favorite treat was apples, I learned. I settled for the warm milk from Mother, which made me stronger by the hour. If I wasn't nursing, I was sleeping.

On my second day, our caretakers came into the paddock, and one put a halter on Mother's face. It made her look weird.

"Why do they do that?" I asked.

"So they can take me where they want me to go," she explained. "Just follow me, Little One. I think we're being taken to the pasture."

The door to the paddock opened, and I followed Mother into a wide area with opened ends. I hesitated, unsure of what to expect. Mother whinnied for me to follow her.

Mother was led by her halter, and I stayed close to her heels. Her hooves made soft clopping sounds on the hard ground. At the doorway of the barn, there was a strange furry creature with whiskers and a long tail.

"What is that?" I asked.

"That is a cat," Mother replied.

"What do they do?"

"They keep our barn free of mice, snakes and rats, and they are good companions to the humans. They like to sit on their laps and be petted."

I passed the cat, which paid me no heed, and stepped out of the barn and into a world that was new to me – sunshine, sky, grass, dirt, birds, bugs, and flies. The enormity of what I saw took my breath away.

The dirt was soft under my hooves and the sun shone warm on my back. I stayed close to Mother's rump. We came to a gate, and the human took off Mother's halter, opened the gate and gently slapped her rump, which sent her running into the pasture. I hurried after her, and the gate closed behind me. The human stood and watched as I bounded after Mother. I jumped for the first time, kicking up my heels, so glad to feel my legs strong and sturdy. Mother slowed down, and I soon caught up with her.

"It's so good to be outside again!" she exclaimed as she kicked up her heels.

"Wow! This sure is a lot bigger than the paddock."

"There is no end to the world," Mother explained as she slowed to a walk. "The sky goes on forever."

"How do you know that?"

"I've been other places, Little One, and the sky was just as vast there as it is here. The world is a very big place, at least that's what I've heard from other horses."

Just then I heard a tremendous pounding on the ground, causing it to shake, and I turned to see a huge horse barreling toward us. Quickly, I hopped behind Mother, my spindly legs trembling with fear.

"Slow down, Thunder!" Mother loudly neighed. "You're scaring Little One!"

The huge horse came to a halt not far from me, and the size of the beast became clearly evident. He looked just like Mother and me, but a whole lot bigger. His coat was shiny, and his mane blew in the wind as his tail trailed behind him when he ran. I was in awe and speechless.

"So this is your new foal," Thunder said as he observed me. "Is it male or female?"

"Female, for which I'm grateful. Males tend to be ornery, like you." Mother shook her head and tossed her mane as she laughed softly.

"Oh, hush, Tinkerbell," Thunder gently chided. "I only pretend to be ornery."

Thunder took a closer look at me. My legs were still shaking. Mother turned and nuzzled me. "This is Thunder, one of the other horses on our farm. He's named such because he makes a sound like thunder when he runs."

I found my voice despite my shaking legs. "But why is he so big, Mother?" My voice sounded squeaky.

"Well, it's not that he's big, but that we are small, Little One," Mother explained. "We are miniature horses, so we are much smaller than most other horses. Humans ride horses like Thunder, but they don't ride us."

"Ride? What's that?"

"They sit on their backs, in a thing called a saddle. They tell the horses to go certain ways by pulling on a bridle, which is something like a halter, and even tell them when to run and walk. But we're too small for humans to ride, unless they are very young."

I looked at Thunder, whose legs were longer than Mother was tall. His chest was massive, his neck like a pillar, his back wide and strong. I instantly understood how a human could ride Thunder.

"If we can't be ridden, what good are we to humans? Why do they have us?"

"We are pets to the humans, companions, sort of like dogs and cats. However, I've pulled a small wagon before with little humans in it, but I haven't done that since I arrived here. So all I do is eat and sleep while the humans brush me and play with me. It's a very good life."

The shaking of my legs had finally ceased. Thunder approached me, and when I didn't pull away, he muzzled my neck. It tickled, and I laughed.

"You'll do well here," Thunder stated. "Just be obedient to our human caregivers, and life will be good."

Mother interrupted. "There are two more big horses just like Thunder that live here – Patches and Buttercup. I'm sure you'll meet them soon."

"Naturally, they're pretty enough, but not as handsome as me," Thunder stated as he pranced around me, stomping his feet and making the earth shake again.

"Not that you're conceited," Mother laughed.

"Well, I still need to run a bit to stretch my legs. See you around, Little One." With a shake of his mane, Thunder turned and thundered down the pasture.

I watched in awe. His black hair glistened in the sun, his mane danced in the wind, and his tail streamed behind him. He was a magnificent sight. Suddenly, I knew I wanted to be like Thunder!

"He's a showoff," Mother stated as she observed Thunder's dash across the pasture.

"He's incredible!" I said.

"Don't let your small stature dictate how you look at life," Mother instructed as she slowly turned and walked to a patch of tall grass and started grazing.

I turned and followed her, hungry again, but the vision of Thunder racing through the pasture was indelibly etched on my mind.

Chapter Two

After filling my stomach, I fell asleep in the green grass; the sun felt good on my hair. It seemed only like moments later that Mother was nudging me, urging me to stand up. I struggled to stand on my gangly legs and heard Mother whinny softly in greeting to two other horses as they approached us. They were big, but not nearly as big as Thunder, who I could see grazing in the pasture along the fence in some shade from a big tree. Mother trotted toward them.

"Hello, Patches! Hello, Buttercup!" she neighed as she touched muzzles with the two horses. "I was wondering where you were. Little One arrived yesterday, and I want you to meet her."

I stood my ground as Patches, who had white, brown and black hair and a white mane and black tail, slowly approached me. "Well, look at you!" she exclaimed. "You're a wee little thing! I'm still amazed that something so tiny can be a horse." She licked my face in greeting, and fortunately, I managed to stay on my feet.

Buttercup, who was golden like the sun, did the same. "Yes, you're small, but you're like a toy to humans, so you're really quite fortunate. We have to work for our keep!" She snorted as her hoof pawed the ground.

"Oh, don't complain," Mother chided. "At least you get to do something that's useful." She came and stood by my side. "Where have you been? I noticed that you weren't in your paddocks or in the pasture when we came out today."

"Oh, we were off 'earning our keep', as Buttercup calls it," Patches stated. "We were put in the trailer and taken somewhere by BossLady...."

"That's what they call our female caregiver," Mother quickly explained.

"....... and ridden in a wooded area on some very nice trails by her and Happyone. It was a nice two days, but I'm sorry that we weren't here to greet Little One when she was born."

I listened attentively, not having anything to say at the moment. Patches and Buttercup seemed like nice horses, just like Thunder, and I gathered that I didn't have anything to fear from them even though they were so much bigger than Mother and I.

"No matter," Mother said. "Things went rather quickly, and Little One arrived as the sun was rising. Boss didn't know it until he came to check on me after the sun was up. We stayed in the paddock the rest of the day and were brought to pasture earlier today."

Buttercup nodded to Thunder in the distance. "So I presume you've met Thunder." Everyone looked at me, and

Mother urged me to answer. Carrying on conversation was new to me, as was everything in my world, and I would have much rather eaten and slept some more in the warm sun than talk to everyone. But their kindness mustn't be repaid with bad manners, so I answered.

"Oh, yes, but I thought he was going to pound me into the ground!"

Buttercup laughed softly and shook her head in agreement. "Oh, that Thunder likes to show off his speed and power, especially to new horses. He doesn't impress us any more!"

"And don't let him scare you," instructed Patches. "He talks tough, but he's really got a soft heart."

"A soft heart, indeed!" exclaimed Buttercup. "I guess we've been good for him because he used to be a real hard-hearted, hard-headed young horse when he arrived here. Do you remember, Patches?"

"Oh, yes, I remember. But I don't really think we had much to do with it, Patches. Don't you remember when he had some body parts removed? Ever since then, he's been kinder and gentler to us mares, and he stopped chasing us and biting us, too."

Mother laughed. "I can't imagine Thunder biting you."

"Oh, but he did, all the time. Of course, that was well before you arrived here."

I nudged Mother and tried to nurse again. I was starving! When were they going to stop chatting and let me eat and sleep again? I whinnied softly to get her attention.

"Well, I'm glad you're back, but Little One is again hungry. She can't seem to fill up! I guess she has four hollow legs!"

"Hollow? What does that mean?" I asked.

Mother laughed softly. "It means that there's nothing inside them, but that's not true. Saying you have 'hollow legs' is just a figure of speech for not being able to fill your stomach."

I shook my head, totally confused. First, hollow legs, now, figure of speech. I realized that I had a lot to learn.

"Come, Little One, to the shade under the tree. The sun's getting hot today," Mother whinnied softly as she started walking.

"We'll see you around, Tinkerbell and Little One. We're glad to have you here."

Mother ambled along the side of the fence with me close on her heels. Suddenly, something flew in front of my nose and startled me, and I fell on my rump. Mother laughed.

"What was that?" I asked from my position on the ground as I watched the colored thing with wings flutter past Mother, who wasn't scared by it at all.

"That, Little One, is a butterfly. Aren't they pretty?" She lifted her nose into the air and watched as it circled around her head. "They like flowers."

Sticking my skinny legs out, I hoisted myself to my feet again, curious as to the thing called a butterfly. "I think they should be called flutterflies," Mother said as she followed the butterfly with her eyes, "because they don't fly straight and fast like birds, but instead bounce around in the air in every direction imaginable."

The butterfly continued its dance around us, and much to my delight, it landed on my nose. "Look, Mother!"

"She must like you!"

Just as suddenly, the butterfly lifted into the air and fluttered across the pasture, and soon I couldn't see it any more. "I hope I see another one. They're pretty."

"You will," Mother stated as she resumed walking. "They fly around here all the time, except when it's cold."

"Cold? What's cold?"

"It's hard to explain," Mother said, "but you'll experience it some day."

After nursing again in the shade of the tree, I crashed and took another nap. Mother grazed and rested. Patches, Buttercup, and Thunder rested, too, in the shade of the trees. The day was warm, the sun shone brightly.

Later that evening, we were ushered back into the paddock, and Thunder, Buttercup, and Patches were as well. I noticed that the paddock had been cleaned and that fresh straw had been spread. I stuck my muzzle into it and immediately sneezed, which made Mother laugh.

Our caretakers, Boss and BossLady, were busy in the barn, scooping out oats and grain to the big horses, but that was of no interest to me. I had my meals, warm and no chewing necessary! Mother, however, eagerly ate her oats and hay that were piled in the corner of our paddock.

As usual, I slept after filling my belly. The fresh straw was fragrant and cushioned my bony frame. Mother had told me that I'd fill out like her but that it would take a few weeks to do so and that I would be able to eat solid food when I got older.

As I lay in the straw, I opened my eyes and watched Mother. She was a very pretty horse – although very small in comparison to the others on the farm. Her coat was brown and shiny, reflecting the soft light overhead. Her mane was almost the color of straw, as was her tail, which draped down from her hind quarters to the ground. She constantly swished it to keep flies off both of us, and I found I liked to stand with my head near her rear to take full advantage of it. My tail, on the other hand, was short and stubby and not very useful. Mother's face was pretty, with a small white blotch between her eyes. Her stubby legs were white from the knees down. Little did I know at the time that we looked exactly the same.

Our routine was quickly established – out to pasture early in the day, where I could run and chase butterflies and birds, sleep in the tall, sweet grass, play with the frogs near the pond – and then back to the paddock when the sky darkened. Our caregivers and their two offspring, Happyone and Strongson, often saddled Patches, Thunder and Buttercup, and I watched as they trotted off across an open field, their tails streaming behind them in the wind. The longing to be big so I could be ridden grew inside my chest on a daily basis.

On one such day, Mother observed me as I watched the big horses trot away with their riders. She gently muzzled me. "I can see that look in your eyes, Little One. You'll never be a big horse. You would be wise to let go of the longings of your heart; if you don't, you'll be an unhappy miniature horse all of your life!"

I turned and gazed at her, the sound of the trotting hooves fading in the distance. "But I can't let go of it, Mother! If I want to be big bad enough, why can't I?"

Mother shook her mane, causing the sun to dance in shivers of light. "You're a miniature horse, Little One; that's what you are, and you can never be anything else. That bush over there," she nodded with her head, "can never be a tree that provides shade for us. It is what it is, and there's no changing that."

I was puzzled. Surely there was a way for me to become a big horse that could be ridden and run like the wind! Surely! I shook my head in disagreement.

"Well, when I get old enough to eat, I'm going to eat all the oats I can, and I'm going to eat grass all the time, and hay, too! I'll get bigger! You'll see!" I bolted ahead and ran as fast as my short legs could go toward the other end of the field, but the burst of energy utterly exhausted me. I collapsed under the shade of the big tree as I watched Mother cross the field toward me at a gentle trot.

When she reached me, she didn't say anything, but started grazing instead. I soon fell asleep, cooled by the shade of the tree overhead and the earth beneath, still convinced that I would one day be a full-sized horse.

Chapter Three

The days passed quickly for me, and each brought a new discovery or experience. Several stand out in my memory, which I do have. Some people think that horses don't remember things, but we most certainly do! Naturally, there are also some things I'd like to forget, but can't.

Anyway, when I was several days old, Mother and I were put to pasture as usual. I noticed right away that the sun was nowhere to be seen. Clouds covered the sky.

Mother went about her business of eating, and I went about my business of nursing and running around like the crazy foal that I was until I crashed on the grass. During my second nap, I awoke to water falling on me. I bolted to my feet on my strong, skinny legs.

"Who's squirting water on me?" I hollered as I looked around for the culprit. Surely Patches wouldn't do such a thing, although I highly suspected that Buttercup was capable of doing so.

I heard Mother laugh. "No one is squirting water on you, Little One! It's raining!"

"Raining? What's that?"

"Water falls from the sky and soaks into the land, providing moisture for the plants and grasses that grow, including those that we eat."

I shook my stubby mane and swished my stubbier tail. "Well, I'm not sure that I like rain!"

"Come," Mother said as she walked toward the barn. "Boss is opening the gate for us to return to the barn."

I trotted beside Mother, shaking myself continually as we walked into the shelter of the barn. Buttercup, Thunder and Patches had not been let out to pasture that day, and I heard Buttercup snicker as I walked past.

"You're silly, Little One!"

"Well, I don't like water falling all over me," I explained as Boss opened the paddock door. Mother went through the gate and received an affectionate slap on her rump, but I jumped through too quickly to be touched.

Mother turned and listened to Buttercup, whose paddock was next to ours, after the door was closed.

"I had my hooves trimmed, as did Patches and Thunder, and then we were given baths."

"I thought you looked nice and clean and shiny," Mother replied.

"What's a bath?" I prodded.

"Well, Boss and BossLady spray us with water from a hose, and then we get covered with soap, which they rub into foam, and then they spray us with water again until all the foam runs out of our hair and onto the ground. It washes out all the dirt and, as you can see, the result is quite nice," Mother explained. "In fact, I hope I get a bath soon; it's been a while, that's for sure."

"I hope I never get a bath; I didn't like the rain, so it's highly unlikely that I'd like a bath!" I firmly stated as I curled up in the soft straw as the hum of raindrops splattering on the barn roof created a soothing sound.

But that wasn't the only sound I heard. Boss and BossLady were talking in their language which, of course, I couldn't understand. After a few minutes, they entered our paddock with a bucket full of things that I hadn't seen before. Mother eagerly walked toward Boss as if she knew what was going to happen, and she muzzled him and snorted softly.

Boss reached into the bucket and pulled out an odd-looking thing and started rubbing it all over Mother. She enjoyed it immensely. As I watched, some of her hair started falling out, but she didn't seem to mind in the least, and the hair that was left became shiny, making Mother look almost as pretty as Buttercup. Mother stood and enjoyed the entire process, which I later found out was grooming, and when her body was done, they took a different funny-looking thing and worked on her mane and tail. I hadn't noticed that it was tangled and full of knots.

Now that I wasn't falling asleep at the drop of a hat, I watched the transformation with wonder. When the grooming was completed and all of those funny-looking things, called combs and brushes, were returned to the bucket, Mother looked stunning. She was given an apple, and when she bit into it, the juice squirted all over the place and she slobbered a bit, but the apple was soon gone. I wondered what an apple tasted like.

BossLady came to me and gently rubbed me down with a soft rag. I wasn't afraid of the humans as I had been when I was first born. I was now used to their presence and their touch. She used the soft rag to rub me down, and I realized that it actually felt wonderful! Thankfully, they left the bucket full of brushes and combs by Mother's side and took them out of the paddock when they left; I don't think I would have enjoyed being brushed or combed just yet.

Mother was soon asleep on her feet, but not me. The straw was my place to sleep, and the sound of the pattering rain gently lulled me into a deep sleep on top of a fresh pile of straw. Most of the time, while I slept, my brain was still going like crazy, and dreams were frequent. I was in the middle of chasing frogs down by the pond when I was frightened awake by an extremely loud noise, the likes of which I'd never experienced. I bolted upright with a start. Mother was awake, too, and she looked at my frightened expression with an understanding nod.

"Don't be afraid, Little One," she softly crooned. "It's just a thunderstorm."

The sky flashed with blinding light, sending me running to Mother's side, and then the earth seemed to shake with ferocious rumbling. Mother turned her head and gently nuzzled me.

"It's okay. Sometimes when it rains, fire shoots through the sky, causing thunder to roll through the hills. It won't harm us."

The trembling in my legs eased a bit with the reassurance of her words. I pushed my head under her belly. "It sounds like Thunder is running in the barn!"

Laughing softly, Mother said, "Now you know why he's named Thunder!"

"When will it stop?" I asked as yet another bolt of light shot through the sky, quickly followed by the crashing noise. I wanted to get away from the noise and light.

"Hopefully, soon. Just be glad that we have a nice dry barn in which to take shelter when it storms. Some horses aren't so fortunate."

"Really?"

"I can tell you that because I know," Mother whinnied. "Before I came to this lovely place, I was owned by other humans who didn't provide very well for me. When it rained, I was often left in the pasture, and although trees are good for providing shade, they're not very good at keeping a horse dry. I used to get soaked to the skin, and then I'd get cold, and then I'd get sick, and the animal doctor would have to come. My frequent illnesses could have been prevented by simply giving me a roof over my head when it rained."

"Why didn't they give you a roof over your head?" I asked. I noticed that the thunder seemed to be moving away, and I began to relax.

"I don't know, Little One. It would make sense, wouldn't it? Here, we're brought in every time it rains, and we don't have to stay out and get soaked and cold. As I said, we're very fortunate."

The sky began to brighten a bit, and I walked over to the window, which was high above my head, and gazed up at the sky. The clouds were various shades of gray, and some streaks of sunshine were beginning to break through cracks in the clouds. The rain had diminished to a light sprinkle, as it had been when we were called into the barn. Mother came and stood by my side. As we craned our necks to look up at the clouds, a band of color appeared in front of the black clouds which lingered on the horizon. I sucked in my breath in amazement at the strange and wonderful sight. Mother saw it, too.

"That's a rainbow! Isn't it gorgeous?!"

"Rainbow," I whispered as I stared in awe.

"Yes, rainbow, and they are rare to see. Our Creator has blessed us today, Little One."

I continued to stare at the awesome sight in the sky until it faded from view. "Where did it come from?" I asked. "And where did it go?"

"That's a mystery, and I don't suppose I'll ever know the answer."

As the rainbow faded from view, the storm clouds moved away, and the sun splashed colors – yellow, orange, and pink – across the sky as it slowly disappeared for the night. I'd never seen such a display in my short life. Oh, I'd seen sunsets before, but this one was by far the most glorious; it simply captivated me.

Eventually, I settled down for the night, tucked in the warm, dry straw, my mother's breathing a comforting sound in my ears.

Chapter Four

Ideally, I wished I could go through life without ever having a bath, but the day finally arrived when I was introduced to the procedure. Mind you, I had no intention of going easily to what I thought would be my undoing, so when BossLady approached me with a bucket, I tried to run away, but I was in the paddock and had no place to go. I knew something was up when Mother was taken from the paddock and I was held back. I'd never been separated from Mother before, and seeing her rump disappear behind the closed paddock door sent my heart racing. What in the world was going on? I wondered.

Only a few minutes later, BossLady came into the paddock and put a rope around my neck, and that in itself frightened me half to death. I'd never been restrained in such a manner, but Mother had told me that having a rope around a neck wasn't a bad thing, that the humans simply wanted us to go with them and that's how they led us. She didn't seem to mind, but when the rope was put around my neck, I panicked and started jumping around like the frogs down at the pond. BossLady, however, spoke softly to me and held the other end of the rope so

I couldn't get away, and before long I settled down and stood quietly, realizing that the rope wasn't hurting me in the least.

Now, the bucket of water was an entirely different matter. BossLady brought it in, dipped her hand in the water, pulled out a sponge full of water and started rubbing it on my chest. I hadn't relished the prospect of being wet despite Mother's and the other horses' seeming enjoyment of the entire bathing procedure. If you remember, I hadn't enjoyed the rain falling on me in the least, and this bathing ritual was certain to get me much wetter!

BossLady was kind and gentle despite my bad behavior. Before long, I decided that I was fussing for nothing, that I wasn't getting hurt in the least, and that stopping my kicking and jumping just might be a wise thing to do. So I did. Bosslady seemed very pleased when I settled down. She ran the wet sponge over my body, and when she was done, she took a dry rag and rubbed me down, which removed most of the water. When she was finished, she pulled a slice of an apple from her pocket – I knew I smelled something, but I didn't know what it was – and held it in her hand. Gingerly, I stepped forward and sniffed it. I stuck my lips on it and pulled it into my mouth, and I had my first food other than what I got from Mother! It was really good, too – crunchy, juicy and tasty! I realized why apples were Mother's favorite treat.

Once my bath was done, I was let out into the pasture with the other horses, and I immediately trotted over to where there was little grass and lots of dirt and took a good roll in the dirt! Mother laughed, which made me laugh.

"You silly baby! You just had your first bath, and now you're getting all dirty again!"

I rolled around on my back, my long, bony legs flailing in the air as I twisted and turned. When I got finished, I stood and shook as hard as I could. Dust enveloped me. I didn't care.

"I was afraid of the bath at first, Mother, but it really felt good, so I'm thinking that if I get dirty again, Bosslady will give me another bath!" I kicked up my hind legs and trotted off toward the pond, where I ran through the water at the edge, splashing myself and everything nearby. Mother couldn't stop laughing.

And so my days went. Life was good, full of sunshine, baths, playing in the water and dirt, and trying to run as fast as Thunder, Patches and Buttercup. Before long, I noticed that Mother was getting smaller, and I didn't understand why.

"I'm not getting smaller," Mother whinnied, "you're getting bigger, Little One!"

"See, I was right!" I hollered as I jumped around her. "I told you that if I ate a lot, I'd grow up to be a big horse!"

Mother eyed me sternly. "Little One, you'll stop growing when you get as big as me. I've cautioned you not to get your heart set on being as big as Thunder because it will never happen."

I shook my mane and raced to the other side of the pasture, where Thunder was grazing. I ran so fast I had a hard time stopping and almost bumped into him. He lifted his head and gazed at me as he chewed a mouthful of green grass.

"Look, Thunder, I'm growing! I thought Mother was getting smaller, but she tells me I'm getting bigger! Someday I'm going to be as big as you! I just know it!"

Thunder raised his head and neighed, and I didn't like the tone of it. He was making fun of me! "You silly little horse, you'll never be as big as me! Where did you get such an idea?"

My heart sank. "But I'm growing every day….."

"Which you're supposed to do," interrupted Thunder, "but you're a miniature horse, just like your mother, and you'll never be as big as me, or Patches or Buttercup, for that matter. No matter how much you eat, that will never happen." He pawed the earth with his black hoof.

My heart did more than sink – it fell to the ground. I hung my head and turned around as I realized that Mother must have been telling me the truth. I was crushed.

I saw Mother standing a short distance away, and I avoided her gaze. I lost my interest in playing that day, but later that evening, I was introduced to something new – real food! I was given a small handful of oats by Boss, and I ate them from his hand. They were good, crunchy and different. I'd been trying a little grass while in the pasture, but most of my food still came from nursing, but I realized, after eating the oats, that my stomach was a lot fuller, so I tried to get Boss to give me more. He laughed at my efforts.

After that, oats became part of my mainstay, and I learned to eat more grass every day. Soon, I wasn't nursing much at all. I grew more every day, too, and soon I was almost as big as Mother. It was a strange feeling to stand shoulder to shoulder with her.

With my growth came the full understanding that I'd never be as big as Thunder. It was hard to take, this truth that I didn't want to accept. My pining did nothing to make me grow any taller, just as Mother had said, and there was a sliver of sadness deep inside me that I couldn't dispel.

Those first years of my life were wonderful. Boss and Bosslady were good to us, and there were several times that Mother and I were put into the trailer and taken to places where small humans petted us until I thought my hair would fall out. The first time we went, I was pretty scared, but Mother assured me that we made the small humans happy by allowing them to pet us, and we did. After the first time, I began to enjoy those outings. Naturally, we were bathed before we were taken, and I got the entire soap ritual that had been explained to me. The days of sponge baths with plain water were over, but getting bathed made me feel pretty, just like Mother.

When the weather turned cold, our coats grew long and thick, providing the warmth we needed to stay outdoors in the pasture when it was cold enough to see our breath. During the cold months, Thunder looked a little ragged with his long coat, and no amount of brushing could make him shine like he did during the warm months. And after the cold weather passed, Boss and BossLady would comb our coats, which shed hair all over the ground. Oftentimes, the wind would pick it up and swirl it around us, which made me kick and jump with excitement. Happyone often came to help care for us, too, and I preferred her brushing me – her strokes were gentler. She didn't live with Boss and BossLady, but came and went in her truck. So did Strongson. I wondered why they didn't live with the Boss and BossLady. I lived with my mother, and I didn't understand why they didn't live with theirs.

And so I lived and enjoyed life with Mother, Thunder, Patches and Buttercup. We were well cared for and enjoyed life immensely. But, unknown to us, a string of events was about to occur that would change our lives completely.

None of us could have seen it coming.

Chapter Five

When the cold weather retreated and my third season of warm weather arrived, our caregivers, Boss and BossLady, stopped coming to see us and take care of us as they usually did. This was very perplexing to all of us in the barn.

"Why isn't Boss letting us out today?" Thunder stomped the first morning Boss failed to come to the barn. "I need to run and stretch my legs!" Thunder's hooves shook the ground as he pranced around his paddock.

"Surely he'll be here soon," mused Patches. "He's always let us out, him or BossLady."

"Well, I'm getting tired of waiting, too," Buttercup stated as she shook her mane and looked out over the gate to her paddock. "This isn't like him to not come. I wonder why he's not here yet."

Since Mother and I were so much smaller, we could run around in circles in our paddock to stretch our legs. It was a bit tricky, but we could do it if we wanted to. Now that I was just as big as Mother and looked just like her, we'd often try to trick Buttercup into thinking that we were each other, and we often confused her to the point where she'd get mad. Anyway, being stuck in our paddock wasn't as bad for us as it was for the bigger horses.

"I don't see Boss's truck," Thunder informed us. "Boss and BossLady haven't come back from where they went yesterday. I wonder where they are."

"That's unusual," Buttercup stated. "They've never gone away and left us like this before. They've always been here to care for us."

"Well, I'm hungry. My oats are gone, and my water bucket needs to be filled, not to mention that my paddock needs to be cleaned out. I can't walk around my poop all day!"

I laughed at Thunder's complaints. "Stop eating so much, and you won't poop so much!"

"Little One, it works like this – big horse, big poop; small horse, small poop! There's nothing I can do about it!" Thunder kicked the paddock, causing the whole barn to shake.

It was well past midday when we saw a truck pull up close to the barn. Since we couldn't see over the paddock gate, Thunder told us what was happening.

"A male human has gotten out of the truck," he told us.

All of us were silent as we listened for the strange human. After several moments, Mother asked, "What's happening, Thunder?"

"Another truck is coming down the road. I think it's Happyone. It looks like her truck."

"Finally!" neighed Buttercup. "She'll let us outside."

"Yes, it's Happyone. She's getting out of her truck now and going over to talk to the strange human. Now I can see who it is. It's Tallman, Happyone's friend." Thunder paused. "Happyone isn't smiling. Her face looks very sad. I wonder what's going on."

"She's always smiling," Patches observed. "Ever since I came here, Happyone has smiled every day. I didn't know she knew how to look sad."

We waited patiently, curious as to the happenings outside our barn. Thunder was the only one who had a good look at the road and where the trucks parked, so he was the one who kept us informed, albeit rather slowly. I, in my youthful exuberance, demanded to know if they were coming to the barn.

"No, they're talking, and Happyone is wiping her eyes. She's making an odd sound, and Tallman is wrapping his arms around her. She certainly isn't happy today."

Thunder was quiet and continued observing Happyone, who wasn't happy for some unknown reason. After a few moments, Thunder said, "Both Happyone and Tallman are coming toward the barn. I think they'll let us out and take care of things."

I heard the barn door slide open, and Happyone and Tallman entered the barn. Our paddock was opened first, and Happyone spoke softly and gently to us. She knelt down and put her arms around my neck, and her eyes shed water onto my hair as she made odd sounds of sadness. It was very strange. I'd never experienced such behavior from her before. I was glad when she stood up and slipped a halter over my head. Tallman had put Mother's halter on, and we were led from the barn to the pasture, where we quickly kicked up our heels and took a quick run. Shortly after, Thunder, Patches and Buttercup joined us, but we were keenly aware that something wasn't right with Happyone. We'd never seen her like this before.

After having a good run down the pasture and back, all five of us stood and watched the barn, hoping that Happyone would start smiling when we saw her again. The sun climbed through the sky, and Tallman and Happyone worked in the barn. Occasionally, they'd bring the wheelbarrow filled with manure out and dump it down a small slope a distance from the barn, but Happyone's face never got happy. Tallman didn't look much happier either. He'd been to our barn on several occasions, and we knew that he was a friend of Happyone, and he was very nice and knew a thing or two about horses, which we greatly appreciated, but he didn't smile that afternoon either.

"This is very strange," Mother noted later in the day. "Boss and BossLady still haven't returned, and Happyone is anything but happy. I don't understand."

If anyone had looked into the pasture, they would have seen five horses, three big ones and two small ones, watching as the two humans cleaned the barn. We had no desire to sleep or to graze, no desire to run through the water in the pond and get all wet, no desire to sleep in the shade of the tree; we only wanted to know why Happyone wasn't happy.

We eventually retreated to the shade of the trees. Late in the day, Happyone and Tallman called us into the barn; we knew that our paddocks would be clean, that there would be fresh hay and oats and clean water waiting for us. The sadness that covered Happyone spilled over to us, and we didn't do our usual running, pushing and shoving that we did on our way to the barn.

Thunder whinnied softly. "It doesn't seem right with Happyone so sad."

I followed closely to his rump, taking full advantage of his tail to rid my eyes of the pesky flies that continually swarmed about. "How can we make her smile again?"

Mother replied, "I don't know, Little One. Surely this will pass and she'll smile tomorrow."

Soon, we were in our cleaned paddocks where we enjoyed our fresh feed and clean water. Later, we heard the trucks that had brought Tallman and Happyone running, and the sound of their engines faded as they retreated down the road.

"They're gone," Thunder informed us. His voice sounded worried, and I was worried, too. Boss and BossLady had never been gone from us this long. If one was gone, the other had stayed at the house; neither of them had ever been away at the same time. All of us were very troubled.

I settled down for the night, but concern for our human caregivers wasn't far from my mind, and I don't suppose it was far from anyone else's either.

When the sun came up the next morning, there was still no sign of Boss or BossLady. Again, Tallman and Happyone eventually came to the house, but it was earlier this time, and we were let out to the pasture earlier in the day. Tallman took care of our needs, while Happyone spent most of the day inside the house. Later that day, Strongson arrived in his truck, quickly followed by several other vehicles and many strange humans, who went into the house. I'd never seen such activity before, and I was troubled and concerned that Boss and BossLady still hadn't returned.

This activity repeated itself for several more days. Our basic needs were attended to, but we weren't groomed as we normally were by Boss or BossLady. Things just weren't right, and we didn't understand what was happening.

Just when I noticed that our hooves were in sore need of trimming, the human who took care of them showed up. That day we were left in our paddocks and taken out one at a time, and Tallman held us while our hooves were trimmed. It was good to know that Happyone and Tallman were taking care of us in the absence of Boss and BossLady, but my heart ached to see them again, to hear BossLady's sweet, pleasant voice as she brushed me.

Even though the house was busy with activity during the day, no one stayed at the house during the nights. The quietness of our existence was confusing. At night, our world was eerily quiet, and the only light was the one that was on top of a tall pole in the yard, but occasionally the moon cast its soft glow across the land.

The days passed, and we settled into a new routine without Boss and BossLady. Strongson, Happyone, or Tallman came every day to care for us, but their faces never looked as happy as they did before the mysterious disappearance of our caregivers. The season slipped into hot summer, with blistering heat and irritating, annoying flies biting at my eyes and legs; the only thing that seemed to keep them at bay was a roll in the dirt or standing next to Mother's rump where I could take full advantage of her swishing tail while she took advantage of mine. The other horses serviced each other the same way, but the flies were pesky and troublesome no matter what we did.

Several weeks after Boss and BossLady disappeared, both Strongson and Happyone came to the house and spent the night. In the morning, they came into the barn and fed us but didn't let us out to pasture. Thunder was upset and stomped furiously. Happyone patted him and hugged his neck as she spoke softly to him. I could hear her soft voice from my paddock. Oddly, she shed water from her eyes onto Thunder's massive neck.

After they left the barn, Thunder pranced around, shaking his mane. "What's going on? Why weren't we let out to pasture? Why am I being kept here?" His snorts and prancing annoyed me, but he wouldn't stop.

"Just take it easy, Thunder," Patches insisted. "None of us like being kept inside all day, but unless you can break down the walls of your paddock, there's not much you can do."

"Something's going on," Thunder announced as he stopped his frantic pacing. "A big truck just pulled into the yard, and there are three strange male humans taking chairs from the truck and putting them up on the yard."

The news had all of us confused. "Is anything else happening?" Mother asked.

"Yes," Thunder replied. "Another truck has delivered more strange humans, and they've gone into the house. Happyone let them in."

"I wonder why all these strange people are here?" Buttercup mused.

Thunder continued after a moment. "And now those strange humans are putting things from the house outside on the grass. Happyone is telling them where to put the things."

"What things?" Buttercup asked.

"They must be things that humans use inside their homes," Thunder surmised. "More stuff is coming out every minute, and more chairs are being set up."

Our barn became quiet as we listened to the activity beyond our walls. Thunder was the only one who could see the activity, and his deep whinnying and soft neighs kept us informed, but his descriptions set fear in our hearts. This was something that was entirely new to us, and none of us knew what it meant.

Before long, many cars and trucks, some pulling horse trailers, arrived at our place and parked wherever they could find a spot. Strange humans of all shapes and sizes arrived and sat in the chairs. Thunder paced, agitated and confused.

As the day wore on, the heat inside our paddocks would have become unbearable, if not for the fans that Happyone had turned on in the morning. Mother and I couldn't see what was going on, but Thunder's descriptions fanned the flames of fear that had set in my heart. I could hear a man shouting in a very strange way, and his voice was louder than I thought a human's voice could be.

The sun was sliding down the other side of the sky when the barn door opened. Happyone came inside, put a bridal on Thunder, and led him from the barn. He swished his tail as he said, "Finally, I get out of here!"

The man started shouting strangely, but then he stopped again. As before, Happyone came in, put a halter on Patches, and took her out, but something wasn't right, and she knew it, too. "I don't like the feel of this, Tinkerbell and Buttercup. Something's going on." She pulled against the lead, but Happyone spoke gently to her and calmed her down. I saw her rump as she passed by my door.

"Mother, what's happening?" I asked. My stomach was in knots.

"I don't know, Little One. I'm as confused as you."

We watched as Buttercup was taken from the barn, leaving only Mother and me. When Happyone entered our paddock, she had two halters, and she slid them over our heads. I tried to be brave, but Mother must have sensed my fear.

"Don't be afraid, Little One. Happyone would never let something bad happen to us."

We were led from the barn and taken down the gentle slope, where Happyone stopped. We were in front of all the strange humans on the chairs. Thunder, Patches and Buttercup were tied up to the pasture fence. Happyone started stroking my neck, but the familiar gesture did little to calm my spirits.

The strange shouting man started up again, and I watched as humans in the crowd held up little signs, but I didn't understand why. After several minutes, the shouting stopped, and the man slammed a hammer down on the table in front of him. Suddenly, all of the strange humans stood. Most of them started walking toward all the items on the ground, but several walked our way. I noticed that humans also walked toward Thunder, Patches and Buttercup, too. I started to pull at my lead. I wanted to break away and run.

"Mother, I'm afraid!"

"So am I, but running away won't help. Try to calm down!"

Thunder's piercing whinny reached my ears. "We've been sold!" he snorted.

"Sold!?" Buttercup fiercely shook her mane as she was untied from the fence. "Where are we going?" She lifted her head high in an effort to pull away from the humans who took her rope, but her efforts were futile.

"What does it mean – sold?" I whinnied softly to Mother.

Mother threw her neck across mine. "It means that we don't belong to Boss and BossLady anymore; we belong to someone else and will go with them." Her neck across mine was comforting.

Thunder's feet shook the earth as he pranced around, his new owners trying to calm him as they stroked his neck. "Goodbye, dear friends," he whinnied. "You've been good companions, and I hope all of us are going to homes as good as this one has been." He stood quietly and looked at me. "Little

One, you're a fine horse, although small, and I wish you the best in life."

I watched as Thunder was led away and loaded onto a trailer. His shiny rump and long black tail were all I could see as the trailer pulled away.

There was so much commotion that I didn't get a chance to say goodbye to Patches and Buttercup, who went with different humans. Mother and I were eventually loaded into a small trailer by a strange man and a strange woman. I was so relieved that we were going together. I don't know what I would have done if we'd been sold to different humans.

"We'll be all right," Mother whinnied as the trailer started to move, swaying and bumping down the dirt road. "We're together, Little One, and that's all that matters."

I looked at her with mournful eyes. I didn't want to be sold; I wanted Boss and BossLady to return and care for us as always.

And so life as I had known it ceased to exist, and another life of a far different nature was waiting for me.

Chapter Six

The ride to our new place was not very long, shorter than the rides we'd taken to stand and let small humans pet us. I watched through the slats of the trailer as hills, trees, and houses sped past, all the while wondering what sort of life awaited Mother and I. My heart banged wildly in my chest. The idea of living under the care of the strange humans in the truck that pulled the trailer was upsetting. I'd known only the kindness of Boss and BossLady and didn't take to the idea of being someone else's responsibility.

Mother whinnied softly, trying to keep my spirits up. "Don't worry, Little One. Horses are sold all the time. This is the fourth time I've been sold, and most of the places I've lived so far have been good, the humans kind and trustworthy. Surely this new place won't be any different." She nudged my back with her muzzle.

"But I'm still scared," I stated as I vigorously shook my mane. "I'm going to miss Patches, Buttercup, and Thunder, not to mention Boss and BossLady. I wonder why they never came home? Why did they stop caring for us, Mother?"

"I don't know, Little One, I don't know, but I do know that things happen that we can't see or understand, and this must be one of those times. Before, when I was very young, the human caregiver that I had stopped leaving his place every day like he usual. This went on for weeks, and eventually, he stopped giving oats to me and the other horses and stopped caring for us. Soon, the hay stopped appearing in our bins, and we started loosing weight. Thankfully, Boss and BossLady bought me, and I've been well fed ever since." She sighed heavily. "Horses don't always understand what goes on in the lives of humans, and we must make the best of what is handed to us. I'm hoping that our new home will be filled with just as much affection as the one we're leaving."

The trailer slowed and turned off the main road and then bounced along a dirt road. I saw buildings in the distance. "I wonder if there are any other horses in our new home."

"I hope so, Little One, but I'm very happy that we're still together."

The bouncing, jostling movement of the trailer finally ceased, and the strange humans, a woman and a man, emerged from the truck and opened the back of the trailer. I looked around and saw a house that was well-maintained, a detached house for the cars, and a small barn. It looked inviting enough, and I signed with relief. Maybe things would be fine, just as Mother said.

No sooner had the trailer gate been opened than several small humans emerged from the house, screaming and running.

The noise scared me, and I pulled against my rope tied to the trailer as I pranced around.

The strange human man, apparently our new owner, said something to the small humans, and they quieted down, much to my relief. I had lived an idyllic, quiet life and didn't know anything else. The chaotic times when we'd been taken to be petted by small humans had been tolerable because Mother had told me that many small humans never got to pet our kind, and we were doing a great service to them by being gentle and allowing them to stroke our hair and rub our muzzles, even though continuous rubbing on my muzzle became quite irritating. But the enthusiasm of these small humans, three in number and all quite small, was a bit different than I had experienced. Apprehension gripped my heart.

The man took Mother's rope first and untied her from the trailer. As he led her down the ramp, the small humans were joined by another woman and man, so I figured that they were the caretakers of the small humans. Mother was quite tolerant of their inquisitive hands and rough petting; she certainly had more patience than me.

The woman who had been in the truck entered the trailer and spoke softly to me as she released my rope. My heart quieted at the gentle sound of her voice. She led me down the ramp to my mother's side, where I, too, had to endure the hands of the three strange small humans. I tried to be like Mother, calm and submissive, but I pranced around and pulled on my lead.

Finally, we were led across the yard, which was shaded by a huge tree, toward the small barn. I took the opportunity to look around further and realized that I saw no other horses. The squealing, jumping children followed us into the barn, and we were led into a paddock that was half the size of our previous one, but it was covered with fresh straw and had a large bucket full of clean water and a bucket of oats awaiting us. Our leads were unhooked from our halters as our new caregivers stood and looked at us. I whinnied softly and approached the woman, who took my muzzle in her hand. Her touch calmed my shattered nerves.

The children kept pushing each other in the doorway, and their parents kept pulling them back with harsh words. I was glad when everyone left a few minutes later and the gate was closed, leaving Mother and I alone. I sighed heavily and closed my eyes. It had been a very long, trying day.

"Well, at least this place looks comfortable enough," Mother observed as she walked around the paddock. "This paddock isn't as large as what we're used to, but I guess it will do."

She walked to the bucket and took a long drink.

"I wonder where Thunder, Patches and Buttercup went," I said as I munched on some oats. "I miss them already."

"So do I, but they'll be just fine, Little One." Mother shook her mane and looked at me. "I was hoping there would be other horses living here, but I guess we're the only ones." She looked sad, a new expression to me. "Some humans don't understand that horses are herd animals; we don't like being alone. We thrive in a group of horses; the larger the group, the better."

"But we'll do okay, Mother, just you and me. We have to."

"I know, Little One, but we'll get tired of not having anyone to talk to but each other. How many interesting things can we possibly say to each other every day?"

We stood quietly for a few moments. The only sound was my teeth grinding the oats. It wasn't that I was hungry; I just wanted something to do that was normal as this had been a very abnormal day after weeks of abnormal days.

Suddenly, our small barn door was thrown open, and the small humans exploded into our barn, shouting and laughing. I jumped and slammed into the wall. The paddock door was pulled open, and the biggest of the small humans came into the paddock. Mother sensed something was wrong and neighed at me. "Stay away from him, Little One! I think he means harm!"

I ran behind her and hugged the paddock wall. The small human grabbed Mother's halter and yanked on it, and she threw up her head in protest. The small human laughed, and the ones standing at the gate laughed, too. I could see that Mother was trying not to hurt the human child even as she tried to protect herself and me.

Mother whinnied loudly, "Leave me alone!" She shook her head fiercely and broke the grasp of the small human, but he laughed and quickly grabbed it again and yanked hard on it. Then he did something that I'd never seen a human do before – he hit my mother on the side of her neck!

"Stop it!" I neighed as I darted back and forth in the confines of the paddock.

Mother's cries joined mine, but the small human slapped her again, causing the other small humans to laugh and point fingers at us. My eyes were filled with terror at such treatment, and Mother's eyes reflected the pain she had endured at the hands of small, strange humans, yet I knew that she could easily and quickly loosen the grip on her halter if she wanted to.

"Mother, don't let him hit you again!"

"I don't want to hurt him!" she neighed back as she stood on her hind legs, which broke the grip of the small human and caused him to leap to the doorway of the paddock.

Suddenly, all three small humans turned and looked as the man who was their caregiver entered the barn and shouted loudly at them. They hurried away, and he came and looked at us before quietly closing the paddock door and leaving us alone. I was shaking from the experience.

Mother stood silently for a moment. When she spoke, I hardly recognized her voice. "Little One, I'm afraid that this place won't be as nice as it was with Boss and BossLady."

"But maybe the small humans don't live here," I said hopefully. "Maybe they live somewhere else."

Mother hung her head. "We can only hope so."

"Are you okay? Does it hurt where they hit you?"

"Yes, a little, but I'll be okay."

We stood quietly, contemplating our new situation and surroundings. The barn had only one window, and it was on the other side of the small barn from our paddock. There was no source of light in our paddock, and daylight quickly faded. Eventually, we heard the small children, the man who was their caregiver and the woman who was their caregiver, leave in a car. Stillness settled on our barn, and we began to relax.

Later, when all was dark, our new owner came into the barn, turned on a light, and spent a few moments with us. It made me relax.

After he left, I said, "Well, it looks like the small humans don't live here, so hopefully they won't be back and won't ever hit you again, Mother."

"I hope so, too. It's been many seasons since I've been slapped by a human, and I never thought it'd happen again."

"Another human hit you before?"

Mother paused before answering. "Yes, many years ago, someone who came to see me before Boss bought me. I was relieved that the man who'd been so harsh with me didn't purchase me but that Boss did instead."

I pondered this bit of information. Mistreatment was something new to me, and knowing that Mother had not been fed by her previous caregivers and had been slapped by our new caregivers planted caution in my heart, caution sprinkled with a bit of fear. The realization that all humans weren't kind settled on me like a damp blanket and made my heart heavy.

We ate in silence, filling our bellies with the oats and hay as we pondered what kind of life we were beginning with these new human caregivers. Exhausted, we eventually fell asleep. I hoped that the future held only good things for Mother and me. Contemplating anything else just wasn't possible.

Chapter Seven

The morning broke with the songs of birds filtering into the barn. Our male caregiver eventually came to the barn, tied a rope to each of our halters, and led us outside, where we were tied up to things stuck in the ground. He tied Mother and me up so far apart that we couldn't touch each other, which I didn't like one bit. I'd been on ropes before, so that wasn't a problem, but being tied up and kept that way, without being able to run and jump and go where I wanted to go, *was* a problem. I neighed softly to Mother after our caregiver returned to his house.

"Mother, what's going on? Why are we tied up?"

Mother looked at me, grass hanging from her mouth. "I'm guessing there isn't a pasture for us to run in, Little One. Being tied up isn't going to be easy or fun for either of us."

"You mean I can't gallop and run fast?"

Mother shook her mane as she looked sadly at me, that sad look that I had noticed the day before. "This is going to be a different life for us."

She went back to grazing, and I did the same, but my thoughts were of my former life and of how great it had been. Grazing gave me something to do as I pondered the seriousness of our situation.

As the sun climbed high in the sky, my thirst became intense, but there was no water bucket around. My rope allowed me to reach only a small section of shade from the massive tree, but the shade moved with the moving of the sun, and I was left in the scorching heat again. Mother, thankfully, was on the other side of the tree and was able to stay mostly in the shade, but she was concerned for me.

"Little One, I wish you could come over in the shade with me."

"Me too, Mother. I'm so hot, and I have nothing to drink. I feel terrible."

"I don't understand why our caregivers haven't provided us with water," Mother exclaimed as she pranced around in agitation. "I'm worried about you, Little One. You need a drink more than I do. At least I have shade. I've got to get their attention."

Mother started whinnying, first softly, then louder and louder until she was neighing, and she peppered her frantic calls with pawing hooves. It worked. Our caregivers came out of the house, the woman first followed by the man. She came to me and said something after putting her hand on my back. The man hurriedly went to the barn and came back with a bucket of water and set it before me. I took a long drink, softly snorting my appreciation. After I'd had my fill of the cool water, the man pulled the stake from the ground and moved me to the other side of the tree where I could get in the shade; however, I still could not get close to my mother.

Mother was also given a drink from the bucket, but the man had to fill it first because I'd drunk so much of it that it was almost empty. The bucket was then left on the ground between Mother and me, and we found that we both could reach it if we pulled our ropes tight and straight. We also found that we could touch each other's muzzles.

And so we remained the rest of the day, tied up under the shade of the big tree, unable to run free and gallop across a pasture. Looking around, I didn't see any pastures that we could gallop around even if we weren't tied up. There was a fence surrounding the yard in which our barn and our keepers' house rested, and beyond that, there were only fields that held no horses or cows. Houses were scattered about at irregular intervals, yet none of them boasted any horses that we could see. This seemed strange to me.

Later, we were returned to the barn and again fed oats. Our paddock hadn't been cleaned, and we had to step around our own business.

The next morning, we were tied up again, but this time, I was put in a place where I could be under the shade of the tree. Still, Mother and I were kept separate. Our owners left for a good part of the day. It was a lonely experience.

"Mother, why do they own us if they aren't going to do anything with us?" I asked as I gazed off in the distance at their retreating car.

"I don't know. I hope that we get to do more than this, for this certainly isn't a good life for a horse."

Unfortunately, with the passing of days, we discovered that one day was pretty much the same as the previous one. Frequently our caregivers would come out and walk us around the yard, and occasionally they'd brush us, but it was a fraction of what was needed. One day, on one of the walks around the yard, I tried to speed up the pace by trotting. The woman was holding my lead, and she started running with me, so I picked up my speed even more and broke out into a full run. I heard her scream, felt my rope jerk tight and fall loose, and when I looked back, the woman was on the ground with the man, who had been leading Mother, hurrying to her side. I stopped, confused as to what had happened.

The man helped up the woman, who was making odd noises and rubbing her knees. I stood still, wondering what to do. I looked at Mother for reassurance.

She whinnied softly. "I think you ran too fast, Little One."

"I'm sorry; I didn't mean to make her fall."

"I know."

The woman slowly came toward me, picked up my lead and held it in her hands. Suddenly, the end of the rope came swinging back toward me, and I jumped to get out of the way, but the rope smacked my rump, stinging me. I flinched in pain. So this was what it felt like to get slapped, either with a hand or with a rope; it really didn't matter. The result was the same. I lifted my head high and walked backwards, away from the woman who, in my eyes, had suddenly become someone to avoid. She spoke harsh words and pulled me toward her. My eyes were wide with terror.

Surprisingly, the woman didn't slap me with the rope again. She rubbed my neck and spoke soft words to me instead as I was led to the paddock for the night, the man leading Mother close on our heels.

After our paddock was closed for the night, I looked at Mother. Her sad eyes reflected my sadness at our situation. What had I done to deserve such treatment? What had Mother done to deserve to be slapped by the small humans? The peace and security that we'd known with Boss and BossLady had evaporated, and we realized that some human caregivers could be harsh.

Mother stuck her muzzle into the bucket looking for oats, but there weren't any. Fortunately, there was plenty of hay, so we had our fill of that, but we sorely missed our oats that evening.

As the days and weeks passed, our spirits were disheartened at the sameness of our lives. The only time there was any variety was when the small humans came over with their caregivers, but that was never anything that we looked forward to. If any of the humans were around, the small humans were very nice to us, but if they were alone with us, especially in the barn, they were harsh and cruel. Mother and I began to dread hearing their voices when they arrived in their car because we knew that we would suffer at their hands if they were able to be alone with us.

Over that season of being alone with my mother, my spirits became very low. Being tied up most of the time was horrid, and my desire to run and kick and jump was continually stifled. Not an ounce of my former life remained, and even Mother was affected by the dramatic change in our circumstances. Gone was the sparkle from her eyes. Gone was the happy whinny at seeing our caretakers. Gone was the joy of running through the pasture in a vain attempt to go faster than Thunder, Buttercup and Patches. Where we used to hold our heads high and happily swish our tails, we now held our heads down low to the ground and only swished our tails to rid our bodies of irritating flies.

The restriction we felt at being tied up was almost unbearable, and it was multiplied by the lack of feed and water to satisfy our bodies. Usually the rains came on a regular basis, but as the weather cooled and the sun slid lower in the sky, days of rain were infrequent, and soon the landscape, especially the pitiful grass under that tree that we depended on so much, simply dried up. Often Mother and I would scratch the powdery earth with our hooves in an effort to find something worth eating, but it was hardly worth the trouble.

One day I noticed that Mother's coat wasn't shiny like it used to be and that her bones were prominent. I mentioned it to her as we stood tethered beneath the tree.

She swung her head around and looked at her backside as she replied, "Yes, I noticed that the other day, Little One, and you're looking the same way." Her dull gaze troubled me as much as the fact that I was looking as poorly as Mother.

I kicked the bucket, empty of water again, in frustration. "Why don't they feed us, Mother!? What is the point of them being our caretakers if they don't take care of us?" I watched the bucket roll in a slow circle before stopping.

Mother's silence caused me to look at her more closely. She looked absolutely awful. She stared at the dusty earth before answering.

"Sometimes I don't understand the ways of humans. It's such a simple thing to feed us, yet it isn't done. My belly is on fire from lack of water, and I've been hungry for so long that I don't know what it's like to be full." Her head hung lower, if that was even possible. "I'm so sorry that you're here with me, Little

One. I wonder what your life would be like now if you'd gone with Thunder or the others."

I stretched my rope as far as it would go and muzzled Mother as I saw a tear slide from her eye. "It's not your fault that we're in this situation. Our caretakers are responsible, not you. Our Creator has given them that responsibility, and yet they choose to ignore it."

The sun beat down through the leaves on the tree as we hung our heads in silence.

And so the days passed. We got enough food and water to keep us alive, but not enough to keep us healthy. We had our hooves trimmed, but only when it became a real necessity. We were brushed infrequently and never bathed. Oh, how I longed for cool water to be sprayed on my back!

Eventually, the leaves on the trees turned color and fell to the ground. The air became crisp and clean, and the sun stayed wherever it went at night for longer periods of time, and when it made its reappearance, it slid lower across the sky as if it didn't have the strength to go any higher. I've often wondered why the sun changes its ways, but I've learned that it eventually gets its strength back and climbs higher in the sky when the leaves start growing on the trees again.

During the winter, Mother and I were confined to our 'barn' most of the time. Occasionally, our caretakers would take us out and walk us around the yard, at which time I was always careful not to run and pull anyone to the ground. One slap was enough for me! The small humans often came over, and we were then tied up in the yard so the small humans could climb on us and ride us, which was decidedly unpleasant. I generally loved making small humans happy, but these were noisy and mean, thoroughly enjoying kicking me in the ribs for no reason at all other than to make me mad. However, we did keep our tempers on those days, but it wasn't easy to refrain from biting one of the small humans or, better yet, giving them a swift kick to put them in their place. But such was not in our nature.

At long last, the sun started its ascent and the leaves started growing on the trees and shrubs again, and the straggly grass under the tree shot up feeble new shoots of growth, which we quickly consumed, but the rains never came. I'd never seen things so dry.

Being tied up wasn't as bad as being kept in the barn, and our spirits were lifted simply by being outdoors with the sun on our backs. Our caretakers were more diligent about providing for our needs in terms of food, although it was still inadequate, but we sorely lacked their companionship, as well as that of other horses.

Bad as our situation was, nothing I had ever experienced could prepare me for what was ahead.

Chapter Eight

One day, when the sun was warm on our backs and the air was filled with the scent of flowers, the small humans and their parents arrived in their truck. The time they were there was normal enough – the usual riding, slapping, and meanness – but something happened when they prepared to leave. I was untied from my stake and led toward the truck.

I threw my head back and whinnied, "Mother!"

Mother neighed back. "I'm sure they'll take me too, Little One! Don't be afraid!"

I was forced to walk up a long side board into the back of the truck. The board swayed under my weight, and when my hooves hit the bed of the truck, I slipped and panicked. I threw my head back and pulled hard on the lead. The grown man who was leading me yanked the rope and pulled me forward. The lead was tied to the truck, and the woman sat down next to me on a bale of straw, which actually did help calm me down a bit. I patiently waited for Mother to come alongside me. Instead, all of the small humans and the grown man climbed into the truck and said goodbye to our caretakers. One of them pulled the board up and slid it into the truck and then lifted the tailgate and slammed it shut. Mother wasn't coming with me!

"Mother!" I neighed. "Help!"

Mother pulled on her rope and ran around in circles, panic in her eyes visible even from my distant point. My belly turned bitter and my heart raced in fear as the truck started moving forward. I kept straining to see Mother under the tree, but she was soon out of sight as the truck rocked and bounced its way down the road and onto a paved road. Soon, her neighs faded as distance separated us. My throat was choked with dust and anxiety without Mother beside me in the presence of those unkind humans.

Even though the ride was short, it seemed like an eternity before it ended. Mother wasn't with me! I was all alone!

When the truck stopped moving, I was led down the ramp and across a lawn that was suffering from lack of water. The earth was dry and cracked. My hooves kicked up dust as I was led away from the small house that wasn't far away. My heart throbbed with anxiety; when would Mother come to join me?

The rope was handed to the oldest human child, and he pulled me – I was reluctant to move – toward a gate, which he opened and pushed me through. When I was on the other side, he removed my lead from my halter and slapped my rear end. I quickly jumped away, not liking the feel of the slap and certainly not wanting any more of them. The human child slid back through the gate and joined the others. They then turned and entered the house, leaving me alone in this new 'pasture.'

It was deathly quiet. Birds were the only creatures I could hear, but their singing did little to raise my spirits.

I turned and perused my surroundings. My 'pasture' was little more than a large yard, some of which bordered the road over which I had just traveled. There was one scrubby tree which would provide little shade, if any. Grass was nonexistent. Weeds infested the ground and were the only plants thriving in the dry earth.

I lifted my head and searched for another horse. There were none! I was alone! But maybe, I thought, Mother could hear me if I called loudly for her. I lifted my head high and neighed as loudly as I could.

"Mother! Can you hear me?! Mother!" My voice sounded strange in the quiet that surrounded me. I strained to hear any reply, but silence was the only thing that greeted my ears. Surely they would return to the other house and get Mother! Surely! How did they expect a horse to survive alone? Horses depend on each other for survival! How could they possibly do this to me?

I took a few tentative steps around my enclosure. There was no sense in calling it a pasture because it wasn't one. I realized that if I ran at a full gallop, even with my small stature, it would take about eight long strides to reach the other side of my enclosure, so my full-throttle runs that I enjoyed so much were still out of the question.

I was thirsty and hungry after my ordeal, but there wasn't any water bucket inside my enclosure, and what little dusty grass there was did little to assuage my appetite. I set about nibbling on the few dried tufts of grass I could find, and it was then that I heard them.

Dogs! Mean dogs! Snarling dogs! Three of them together entered my enclosure, crawling under the fence and running at me with teeth bared! I bolted across the enclosure and turned to avoid crashing into the fence, and the dogs were right on my heels! I kicked and neighed and snorted as I tried to fight them off, but they persistently bit my legs and barked at me. I called out to Mother! I needed her!

Just when I thought I'd be severely injured by the snarling dogs, the male human emerged from the house and called them. Thankfully, they obeyed his command, although reluctantly at first, and they left me shaking and quivering from head to hoof. I huddled in the corner near the road, terrified to expose my hind end to the nasty creatures should they return.

The male human came over to the fence that surrounded my enclosure and motioned for me to come to him. I obeyed, hoping that some form of kindness would be forthcoming. When I reached him, he stroked my mane and neck and patted me affectionately, speaking to me as he did so. I began to relax.

After a minute, he left me and went into a shed close by and returned with a bucket of water a moment later. He placed it in front of me. I was so grateful; I nickered my thanks as I sucked up the refreshing liquid as fast as I could. I drank the entire contents, and he took the bucket and refilled it, leaving it for me when he returned to the house.

I strained my neck. The dogs had vanished. I listened again for my mother calling me, but heard nothing. I heard the humans laughing in their house, but no one came to see me and put me in my stall for the night. I began to realize that I might not even have a stall or a shed to cover me in foul weather as I looked around at the small shed that was close by. Even though I was small, it appeared to me that the shed was totally inadequate for even my small stature, much less a normal-sized horse.

The birds stopped singing and the crickets began chirping as night settled in. My heart was so heavy – Mother hadn't been brought! Would she ever come? Would I be left alone with these horrid small humans and nasty dogs?

My eyes grew moist with tears as I contemplated my new circumstances. It was clear to me that I wasn't in a good place.

* * * * * * * * *

The morning dawned after what seemed like the longest night of my life. With no other horses beside me, I'd heard every night creature as if for the first time, and fear had gripped my heart with each strange noise. Fearful that the dogs would return, I'd hardly closed my eyes the entire night. I was glad when the sun reappeared.

I watched as the small humans came out of the house and climbed into a huge orange vehicle that took them away. I learned that this was a daily ritual, and I was glad when they left because I was free of their unkind treatment until they returned. And they always returned later in the day, when the big orange vehicle groaned its way up the hill to the house, disgorging its contents along the side of the road. Often the small humans came into my enclosure and petted me briefly, and occasionally they'd spend some time with me, brushing me, although they didn't know how to do it properly. Once in a while, one would fill my water bucket, but never did one bring me a bucket of oats or grain for my persistent hunger. The large male human – I can't bring myself to name him or call him a caregiver – did bring me one bale of hay after I'd been there several days, but never did another one appear to take its place when I had consumed it.

Other days, the small humans, especially the biggest one, were unkind, entering my enclosure and slapping me and chasing me. The big one also liked to try to climb onto my back, and I learned to tolerate his attempts in order to avoid being slapped on the neck. I had no way to escape. When he was on my back, he'd kick my ribs and slap my neck to make me run, but running in such a small space was dangerous, not only for me, but for him, but I find it difficult to believe that he saw any danger in it at all. Always, after such treatment, I was left alone.

Day after miserable day, the heat of the sun beat mercilessly down on my back. The lack of water and feed was taking its toll on my coat, which was shedding hair daily even as my weight dropped continually. Soon, I noticed that my ribs were prominent. I was slowly becoming weak from hunger and lack of water.

Rain was non-existent. It was as if the sky had forgotten to rain on the land. The cracks in the earth under my hooves grew wider each day. The heat was almost unbearable, and the paltry speck of shade I had was useless against the continual assault of the sun.

Being alone presented a variety of problems which I'd never encountered before. I longed for the talk of other horses, but I couldn't so much as see one in the distance from my enclosure even though I searched every day. I'd long ago given up calling for Mother; it was pointless and sapped my energy. My eyes were constantly being bitten by flies because Mother's rump with her tail swishing the flies away wasn't next to my face. My eyes became painful and my vision became clouded. I didn't understand what was happening. My hooves were in terrible need of trimming, but I knew that if my human owners wouldn't provide basic needs of food and water and shelter for me, it was highly unlikely that they'd get my hooves trimmed.

Thankfully the lack of rain kept away hoof problems that occur when a horse is forced to stand in water constantly.

The dogs were a constant worry for me. They frequently chased me and nipped my legs, and I knew that I'd never be able to lay down for fear that I couldn't get up in time if they attacked me. The quiet, happy, secure life that I'd know with Thunder, Buttercup, Patches, and Mother was a distant memory, and every day was now a struggle to find food – which wasn't possible in my enclosure – and to keep the small humans and nasty dogs away from me.

The sun crawled across the sky every day as it burned my back and parched the land even further. Only the trees were green, but even they were covered with dust, and many leaves were turning brown and dropping to the ground. Dirt and dust were constantly in my nostrils as I foraged the dry earth for the smallest pieces of dried-up grass. Oh, how I longed for sweet hay and crunchy oats and fresh water! I longed to be brushed and bathed, things I loathed as an ignorant foal! Every muscle in my body ached; my eyes itched and burned from the constantly-biting flies. I had no way to rid myself of the horrible insects, no tail from another horse to assist me. My head hung lower each day as my strength ebbed away. Not only was my body suffering, but my spirit was suffering even greater, I do believe, because I had no other horse for company, no other horse to nudge and brush against, no other horse for conversation. It was a horrid existence. I wasn't living – I was struggling to survive when I should have been cared for by my 'caregivers'.

Thoughts of Mother were never far from my mind. Occasionally I would dream about her and the wonderful times we'd had together when I was a young thing. I especially loved the way she had called me "Little One", but that time seemed so long ago, so detached from the world in which I now lived. Wondering if Mother had been taken somewhere else consumed my mind – hopefully she'd been taken by other humans who would love her and care for her as Boss and BossLady had done. Dreams and hopes for something better kept me alive as the heat and lack of rain continually parched the landscape for as far as I could see as the weeks passed.

The dogs occasionally got the best of me when the humans were gone. I suffered bites in my pasterns, but I must say that I got in a few good kicks once in a while, which made me feel better even though I didn't do much damage. Discovering that the will to survive caused me to do things I normally wouldn't do was an eye-opener. Thoughts that Mother wouldn't be pleased were pushed aside; surely she'd do the same thing in such a situation.

As time passed, the humans stopped by my enclosure less and less. Even the small humans lost interest in me. It was as if I didn't exist. With no food and water, my body became a shell of its former self. My hair fell out. My stomach didn't know what it was like to be full. I gnawed the wood railings of my enclosure, desperate for some nourishment. My belly burned with thirst and the dust coated my throat, causing me to gag and cough constantly. My spirit was broken. I lost hope.

One day, I knew that my time to sleep eternally had come. Thunder had told me about dying, that every living thing eventually dies and that you simply lay down, fall asleep and don't wake up again. I clearly wanted to die. Apparently, it was the only escape from my misery. Life wasn't worth living any longer. I had no strength left. My body was nothing but skin and bones. I could hardly stand upright on my knobby, scabby legs. My eyesight was gone; everything looked hazy out of one eye, and I couldn't see anything with the other. I was of no use to anyone. No one wanted me. My human owners paid absolutely no attention to me. Yes, it was time to go to sleep forever.

And so I walked to the side of my enclosure that ran parallel to the road, and there I collapsed in a heap of despair. I knew that I'd never have the strength to get up again and hoped that the dogs wouldn't find me until I had closed my eyes in that final sleep I desired. I was so weak, so tired, so thirsty and hungry.

I laid there for a while, holding my head up, but soon even that position was too much for my emaciated body to maintain. I laid my head down on the dry earth, the dust billowing in front of my nostrils with each shallow breath. I wondered how long it would take me to go to sleep for the last time. The world didn't seem real any more. I felt as if I was floating somewhere as visions of running with Mother, Thunder, Patches and Buttercup flooded my mind, washing me in peace.

And then the worst possible thing happened – the dogs found me! My peaceful state of mind evaporated in a faint heartbeat as terror gripped me. All three of them ran at me, biting me, nipping at my ears and legs, barking incessantly. I didn't have any strength with which to fight them. I felt my ears being torn, felt my flesh, what little there was of it, being bitten by sharp teeth and torn from my body. I whinnied with my last ounce of strength as fear gripped my heart.

"Leave me alone!" I kicked my legs, but my kicks had no power and found no flesh to contact. "Go away!"

The effort took all my remaining strength. My cloudy eyesight faded into blackness, pain piercing every fiber of my body. The snarling dogs were the last thing I remember as I closed my eyes in sleep. My last thought was that my misery was finally over.

Chapter Nine

Mother had told me that strange things often happen in life, and what happened next most definitely fits into that category.

My long final sleep was interrupted by movement, which I found very odd. My whole body was moving, and I heard the sound of a car that humans ride in. I thought I must be dreaming, but I was aware of the same thing several times as I drifted in and out of sleep. Human voices penetrated my mind, voices I didn't recognize, and in my weakened condition, I couldn't process what was happening.

Following are quotes from USERL's website postings: August 15, 2007 – USERL received a call from officials asking assistance for a miniature mare being seized immediately due to her life-threatening condition. Transportation was arranged immediately to a USERL clinic. USERL investigators arrived at the shelter and evaluated the small mare. The plan had been to transport her to a private equine hospital for immediate care and treatment. However, the mare was lifeless and unresponsive and obviously needed critical 24-hour care. Phone calls to the waiting veterinarian confirmed the need, and it was decided to take her to NCSU College of Veterinary Medicine. She was named 'Sassy' because she must have some sass to still be alive in this condition.

At NCSU, Sassy was put in isolation due to the possibilities of viral infections that could be contagious to other animals and possibly humans. Both of her eyes were ulcerated and infected with damaging scarring on her left. She also has bite wounds on her body and an ear that is damaged and split.

My time of sleep must have been extended because when I woke up, I was in a clean paddock full of deep straw. I thought I was in horse heaven! The smell alone was incredible! Every time I awoke, I smelled the fresh scent of clean straw, and, even in my muddled state of mind, I began to realize that I was in a different place, not back in my enclosure with vicious dogs snapping, snarling and biting me and mean small humans waiting to torment me. Even though I couldn't see much when I was awake because my eyesight was almost gone from the nasty fly bites, I saw shadows of humans moving about and kneeling around me, and I felt gentle hands stroking my mane and bony sides. They were the kindest, gentlest hands I'd felt in a very long time. I often felt my head gently lifted and placed on something soft, and I began to want to live – I wanted to see Mother again.

As time passed, I became aware of a soft blanket cushioning my bony body and cool drops of liquid being dripped into my eyes and patches being placed on them, which didn't bother me since I couldn't see anyway. Gradually, my groggy mind somehow was able to understand that I was now in the care of humans who were helping me.

I don't remember much about my first night at this strange new place, but I do remember a human being with me all the time, even during the night. Someone was always lying down beside me in the straw, keeping me warm and safe. As morning dawned, I began to be more aware of my surroundings and noticed that tubes were sticking out of me in several places. I could see out of only one eye, but not clearly at all; the other one was covered with a patch. My gentle caregivers, two female ones, eventually helped me hold my head up, and I have to admit that it took all my strength to hold it and not flop back down on the straw.

At that moment, I knew that I would make it, that I wouldn't go to sleep forever and die. I wanted to live! These kind humans had given not only my body, but my spirit also, a second chance, and I desperately wanted to get well enough to stand and run again!

Holding my head up caused the humans to make all sorts of strange noises, but I think they were glad for me. One of them placed a bowl of something in front of me; it was mushy, but it was food – real food! – and I ate it as quickly as I could! It tasted so good!

The rest of my first day in this marvelous place was spent sleeping and eating small bits of food. Even though I wasn't able to eat much at one time, I felt stronger every time I woke up. I also seem to recall being sponged and brushed and having my mane braided. The touch of kind human hands was like water on dry, thirsty land! I soaked up every touch!

August 16, 2007 – She was watched carefully overnight and showed little improvement. But late this morning, Sassy began to respond to her caregivers and was helped into a sternal position. She was then given a small bran mash, which she amazingly gobbled down!

My second morning at this wonderful place, I was moved to a different stall, and I could hear other horses! I was so excited that I nickered! After having my morning mush, I was lifted onto my legs by my caregivers. It felt strange standing after being down for so long – I have no idea how long it's been – but it was wonderful. Horses can't be down for long or we can develop health problems. Standing was shaky business that morning, but I stood as my legs shook and my caregivers helped support me. After a few minutes, I was back down on the straw and sleeping again, but every time I awoke, I watched the strange occurrences around me as best I could with my cloudy sight.

As I said, I could hear other horses, and occasionally I'd catch a word or two being exchanged. All the talk was about sickness! How strange! Eventually, I learned that all of the horses that were in the barn with me were sick because they had been mistreated by their caregivers! The information upset me terribly! I pushed it out of my thoughts so I could concentrate on getting well.

While I was resting, I felt a sharp pain shoot through one of my eyes, and I nickered in pain. A caregiver was quickly by my side, and more cool drops of liquid were dripped into both of my eyes. Even though I felt the liquid, I couldn't see anything out of the eye that was so painful. I didn't understand what had happened, but I assumed it had been caused by the flies and my inability to keep them off my eyes by standing next to another horse's rump. My aloneness in my difficult situation had caused the loss of sight in my eye.

August 17, 2007 – Sassy was moved out of isolation since infectious virals have been ruled out as a cause of her condition. She cannot regulate her own glucose levels at this time, so is on an IV infusion pump to regulate it. Her left eye ruptured today due to the ongoing infection. Thankfully, her right eye should respond to treatment and heal fine. Sassy still cannot regulate her own glucose, but it is hopeful that she will start regulating herself once she has regular meals for several days. She's improving daily, standing for 5 minutes this morning! Updates will be posted daily during her intensive care.

Even though I felt much better than when I arrived at this wonderful place, I knew that I was still terribly ill. Wonderful humans were taking good care of me, and I knew that I wouldn't die – at least, I hoped I wouldn't go to sleep forever – but I was disturbed that my eyesight was gone in one eye and almost gone in the other. At least the pain was greatly reduced with the care I'd been receiving, but not being able to see saddened me.

Holding my head erect took all of my energy, and without the help of these kind humans, I wouldn't have been able to hold my head up at all. They would lift my neck and help me get comfortable, and then they'd feed me the mushy food. Every time they brought me a bowl, I'd eat it as fast as I could. I was still literally starving! However, I couldn't eat too much at once, and I think that's why they fed me in small portions several times a day.

Even though I was still very weak, I voiced my thanks to those wonderful humans with nickering and soft whinnies. When I wasn't eating, I was resting flat out on the straw, covered by a blanket that kept me warm. Even though it was the warm season, I found it strange that this new place was cool, and I appreciated the blanket that was tossed over me every time I rested. I didn't have any body fat to keep me warm, no muscles to help me stand and hold my head up, but the food helped me get stronger every day.

With my limited eyesight, I could see tubes that ran out of a bag hanging on the wall and toward me. I didn't know where they went, but I discovered that when I moved, I felt a tug along the side of my neck.

August 18, 2007 – Sassy is holding her own with no improvement nor decline in her condition. She is still eating great and sitting up sternal for spaces of time before laying out for naps. Her glucose levels are still up and down, but not as much as the previous day. She is now on IV nutrition as well, which should also help with her glucose levels over the next few days. Thank you to the clinicians, staff and students of NCSU! They are wonderful with their care of Sassy.

Just when I thought I was getting better, I developed a lot of pain in my stomach, which felt like a ball of fire! I whinnied to the humans, and they soon noticed that I was in distress. I knew the problem, but it took them a while to figure out that I couldn't move the food through my system and eliminate the waste. My body had become so accustomed to starvation that the introduction of food had caused me to become constipated. All of the food I'd eaten since my arrival was stuck in my bowel and I couldn't eliminate it. Again, this was also caused in part by my inability to be on my feet and to move around.

After quite some time, my pain became intolerable, and the humans were clearly aware of my acute distress. They talked among themselves, and one human knelt behind me and pushed something into my rear end. Now, this might not be something to talk about, but it's part of my story, part of my suffering, and the medicine that was stuffed into me – literally – did the trick. Not long afterward, I was finally able to move the waste out of my body. The humans that were with me at the time cheered and shouted and clapped their hands. I found it quite amusing that one of the body's natural functions could create so much excitement!

After my manure was cleaned up and carted away, I was again situated in a sternal position, and I let my caregivers know that I was hungry and that they'd better feed me! Manure out, more food in! I neighed softly, not having the strength yet to be loud enough to shake the rafters, and didn't stop until my daily mush was set before me.

I must have amused the humans a great deal because they were constantly laughing at me, but it didn't bother me. How could I be anything but happy? These wonderful humans had found me and brought me to a place of safety and were caring for my many needs, sitting with me, sleeping with me, and bathing me in kindness! I often wished, during this time, that they could understand horse language for I wanted desperately to tell them of my extreme gratitude. Instead, I showed them by leaning into their gentle strokes and nuzzling them with my nose. I hoped they understood.

August 19, 2007 – Sassy started out with a good day, but then became painful by midday. It was feared she was colicking, but it ended up being a small impaction of her bowel (constipation) and resolved with enemas. Even after all the drama, Sassy was assisted to a sternal position and demanded food! Her endearing perseverance and nickers for attention continue to grab on to all who meet her....

I slept well most nights. My belly was full and I had no worries of being attacked by dogs, so sleep came easily. With each new day, I felt myself getting stronger, and I yearned to be on my feet and to walk around, but I knew that was impossible in my current condition.

Often, I dreamed of Mother and our wonderful times together with Thunder, Patches, and Buttercup as we raced through the pasture, trying to avoid the clods of dirt flying from their hooves as they ran ahead of us. My dream of growing big like Thunder had been lost somewhere, and I'd begun to understand that I'd never be a normal sized horse. My current goal was not to be big, but to live, to stand, and to run again.

With the dawn of another day, I felt pretty good. I ate my mush as usual and stretched out to digest my food. One of my regular caregivers came to see me, and soon others joined her. It was wonderful being the center of attention, being stroked and petted and gently rubbed. I loved the attention lavished on me by all these wonderful humans who really cared about me; it was difficult for me to grasp that they really cared about me after the mistreatment and neglect I suffered.

Despite my wonderful care, my right eye, the one that had some limited sight, became more painful and swollen. My caregivers were very attentive to this situation, but their constant attention to my right eye caused me a great deal of concern. I just wanted the pain to go away and to see well again.

Even though I tried my best to get better, I had another setback. My health issues were numerous, and my body was unable to recover from starvation, dehydration, wounds, and infections all at once. The caregivers that were present when I went into distress again huddled around me, comforted me, and encouraged me. My spirits sank. No amount of willing me to recover could make me recover. Looking back at what I'd endured and the condition I was in when they found me made me realize that it was a miracle that I was still alive; the setbacks and unexplained problems lowered my spirits, but I refused to give up. I would get better!

August 20, 2007 – Another good day began for Sassy today. When I visited with her she was, as usual, sitting sternal and eating her "mush" – a good recover from her ordeal yesterday. Others also dropped by to check on her and found her alert and responsive. However, at the end of the day she was, again, in distress. I have not heard any news tonight (no news is good news), so we are hopeful it is once again a small setback in her recovery.
Another complication today was her right eye. Her left eye is already lost to the infection, but her right eye – although in serious condition – was thought to be salvageable. Today it

shows signs of increased fluid from the infection. Our fingers are crossed that she doesn't lose this eye as well.

I slept fitfully, moving about constantly. I didn't know what was wrong; I just knew that I didn't feel right. When morning dawned, my spirits were still down, so I was quieter than usual, not neighing for my mush and making a ruckus when anyone came to see me. I wanted to see the sunshine again, to smell and eat fresh green grass! But when would I be well enough to go outside? My caregivers were the best, but they couldn't do anything to ease the longings of my heart.

Missing my mother was most painful. I constantly wondered what had happened to her, if she had stayed where I last saw her, or if she'd been taken somewhere else, which meant that she could be in a better place or a horrible place like I'd been. Longing to feel her muzzle against mine, I rubbed my nose through the straw under my head as I closed my eyes and relished the memories with my mother. My heart ached for her.

After my long nap, two of my caregivers tried to turn me over on my other side, which I couldn't do without assistance yet, and surprisingly, I struggled to my feet. It felt so good to stand up, even though it was for a short time; my legs were still weak and shaky. When I went down again, they assisted me into a sternal position and fed me that wonderful mush. I tried to show my appreciation, but my heart was still heavy with longing for Mother and the outdoors.

My eyes were attended to as usual; I slept as usual; I was lavished with attention as usual – but still my spirits were low. I think my caregivers were concerned for me because I wasn't my usual obstinate self. Mother used to call me Little One, but my caregivers are all calling me Sassy, so I guess that's my new name – until I find Mother again, at least.

August 21, 2007 - Sassy made it through the night and was doing better this a.m., but quieter than usual.....Upon arrival, I did notice her more quiet. But when we went to move her to her other side, she struggled and stood well. She was then put into a sternal position for her lunch, which she ate great as usual – and seemed overall more alert the longer she was up – but not as alert as she has been. The source of her distress late yesterday is still unknown, but septicemia from her eye infections is suspect for now. There was no change in her right eye today. The wonderful support for Sassy has been great! And as long as she continues to fight and enjoy her mush, we will give her time to tell us what she wants....

Rough nights seemed to be the norm for a while. Sleep was elusive, and I didn't feel well, but I didn't know why. Not being able to stand for any length of time was probably the reason, but I wasn't sure. Dreams of former better days were constant, but often I'd dream of the horrible small humans and the snarling dogs and would wake up shaking. I was always glad to see the sky lighten with the rising of the sun.

After eating my mush, I stood again, and this time for longer. That alone lifted my spirits. My caregivers were always there to support me and rub me down, which further lifted my spirits.

I was up and down several times that day. I felt my strength returning, and my legs grew stronger every time I made the effort to stand. Of course, I was still not able to get up without help from my caregivers, who steadied me and stood by me, but I spent a great deal of energy doing something that should be easy.

Another reason for my spirits rising was my right eye; it didn't feel so swollen, and I could see light and objects out of it – not clearly, but I could see. I didn't think I'd ever get used to seeing with just one eye, but as long as I had sight in one eye, I determined that I'd make the best of it.

Oftentimes, I'd hear humans I've never heard before, both large and small ones, and I'd see them looking through the paddock slats. They'd always stay and watch for a while, and if I was close enough, I'd allow them to pet me. At first, I was a little wary of the small humans, but after time, I realized that they meant me no harm, and there was always a large human with them. These visits by strange humans were almost a daily ritual. I eventually looked forward to them.

August 22, 2007 – Sassy had a rough night last night, but then became more responsive and alert than ever before today. She stood several times today and continues to eat her meals very well. Her right eye also looked better today, not as swollen. She continues to baffle everyone with her ups and downs, but many are hopeful that her great day today is a turn in the corner for her.

Finally, I had a good night's sleep – no bad dreams and no discomfort. I felt refreshed in the morning and eagerly ate my mush. I neighed at my caregivers and muzzled their hands when they sat with me. I felt really good for the first time since my arrival – not to mention the many weeks before my arrival.

When my caregivers urged me to stand, I got up more easily than ever, and I surprised myself by walking around my paddock! Not quickly, mind you, but tentative little steps, slowly around my space. My shaking legs settled down, and I mustered all my strength to stand as long as possible. My caregivers were delighted! I had to be careful and not walk far as I still had those tubes hanging down and going into the side of my neck.

After my adventure walking around, I napped a long time. I was exhausted. But again, I got up with assistance, not one more time, but twice, and every time I stood, my legs were stronger and my steps were surer. Relief washed over me that I had finally reached this point in my recovery. It had been a long, hard road.

When I was left alone, I'd nap a lot, but when I awoke, I longed to be on my feet again, but there was no one to help me get up, so I tried to do it by myself. I just couldn't manage it on my own, but I gave it a good try and expended a lot of energy, so

I think I napped more that day than ever. But I had walked! I was so very happy!

August 23, 2007 – Sassy had a great night last night, standing (assisted) and then staying up and walking around for three 1-hour intervals. Now that she's been up and can walk, she struggled throughout the morning to get up on her own. She was quite tired from the exertion and napped off and on throughout the day, but still sat up eagerly to have meals. Her right eye is still the same – no progress or worsening of its condition. Sassy is much more alert now, too, nickering when approached and responding to voice and touch very good again.

We are so thankful for the wonderful staff and techs at NCSU that are doing such a great job with her. Her willpower has affected many, and she has quite a fan club now. Due to her popularity, she is now restricted from visitors so that she may rest quietly when she needs to so as to gain strength. USERL is grateful for all the support and well wishers that have come by thus far to cheer Sassy on in her battle. We will continue to update her condition daily on this website so everyone supporting her can be involved in her recovery.

Chapter Ten

Every day was the same, but different, if that can be so. I had a routine of eating, napping, standing and walking, and simply resting as my caregivers fussed over me. I tolerated my eye drops and medications well since I had learned that nothing really harmed me and was probably for my benefit.

However, one day was drastically different. The tubes that were in my neck were removed. It hurt and I jumped when they were pulled out, but the pain quickly subsided. I never did understand what they did, but I presume they were part of what I needed to recover from my ordeal.

Shortly after the tubes were removed, one of my caregivers gave me a wonderful surprise – pieces of an apple! It was a bit of heaven! Even though I thoroughly enjoyed my mush, it was the same thing every time, and having something different was delightful. The apple crunched and squirted juice in my mouth as its sweetness slid down my throat. I whinnied and nickered my pleasure and kept nuzzling my caregiver in thanks, which caused her to laugh and stroke my face and mane. I couldn't get enough of the apple – it was gone all too quickly! Even though this was a joyous occasion, it brought a brief stab of sadness to my heart as I remembered that apples were Mother's favorite treat.

August 24, 2007 – Sassy is still continuing to very slowly improve. She now sits up on her own and is standing for longer and longer periods of time. Her right eye has not worsened (or improved), but stayed as is for several days now. Hopefully, the meds are working and the infection is turning around. Only time will tell....
Due to her improvements, it's been decided to remove IV nutrition to see if Sassy can stay stabilized on her own. If she cannot, then it is unlikely she will be able to do so. If she does, then she's conquered a huge obstacle.
Sassy was her usual "sass" self today and ate very well. She especially enjoyed some cubed apple bits that a caregiver gave her at lunch time (her reaction was delightful) and good scratches in her itchy places.

My days were no longer spent lying on the straw, but standing up most of the time. My legs had gotten strong enough to hoist my still-bony-frame upright, which delighted me to no end. Hopefully, I would have fewer health issues since I could stand up most of the time. My slow walks were no longer hindered by the tubes that had been in my neck, so I was able to explore all corners of my paddock and stretch my neck out and see what else was going on around me.

I'd been most curious about the other horses in the barn, but talk was rare as all of us had physical issues with which we were dealing, so I enjoyed the silence while yearning for conversation with others of my kind.

Finally, I was moved from the paddock where I had been since I arrived, put into a trailer, and taken to another place. At first, I was afraid that it wouldn't be a good place – what could possibly compare to the wonderful place where I'd been? – but I discovered that I had nothing to fear. I walked out of the trailer on my still wobbly legs, across a dry grassy patch, and into another barn. I relished the wee bit of sunshine that fell across my back in the short trip and enjoyed the sky overhead.

Once in my new paddock, I slept. It had been an exhausting trip. Ordinarily, such a short trip would have me running around at my destination, but my strength was far from what it had been. When I awoke, I stood on my own, which I was finally able to do on a regular basis, and immediately started eating the hay and oats that were waiting for me. It was quiet here. I immediately knew that I would be safe.

Shortly after my nap, some nice humans entered my paddock and brushed me and sponged me down. I can't tell you how wonderful I felt! I whinnied to them and nibbled at their clothes as they pampered and groomed me. Memories of my younger days came flooding back at the gentle touches of my caregivers, days when I was groomed and pampered on a regular basis by Boss and BossLady. I sighed heavily. I still missed them, as well as Mother, but I was in a good place, and that was all that mattered for the present.

August 26, 2007 – Sassy was discharged from the Vet School today after successfully coming off the IV Nutrition. She not only remained stable but continued to improve. Sassy can now get up by herself whenever she wants, and stays up for 6 hours or more. Her curiosity about all that she sees is charming. Upon arriving at the rehab farm, Sassy was groomed and pampered while she ate (and she eats all the time). Sassy remains under close supervision as she is not out of the woods yet. But what a remarkable will this girl has shown us thus far! Many thanks to NCSU Vet School for their wonderful care of her! And many thanks to all that have donated for her costly care. Her needs are still costly (eye meds, and a surgery to remove her left eye when she is strong enough), so continued donations are appreciated for her care.

On the first full day at my new home, at least that's what I liked to call it, I was let out to pasture! Grass beneath my hooves, even though it was sparse, short and decidedly dry, was an absolutely amazing feeling! Eating the grass was even better! I'd had my fill of mush! Now I could finally graze with other horses.

Seeing was still difficult for me, but I had one eye that was pretty good, allowing me to make out large objects and shapes. I could even see when my caregivers came at me with things that stuck into me, which made me jump! And I never got to sleep for long stretches as I was awakened, even during the night, at regular intervals for medications and drops. I'll be so happy when I get well.

On my first day out to graze, I was a bit wobbly on my legs. They still weren't as strong as they used to be. I had to stop and think about how to graze and how to place my hooves and legs. I felt pretty ridiculous, really. As I grazed, one of the other horses called out to me with a definite laugh in her voice.

"Hey, what's your name?"

I slowly ambled over to the fence, eager to speak to one of my kind.

"My mother used to call me Little One, but my new caregivers call me Sassy," I answered. "What's your name?"

"Dreamer."

"You're the first horse I've been able to talk to in days and days," I said as I reached the fence that separated us and lifted my head up to hers.

Dreamer stretched her muzzle to mine. "You're a tiny thing, that's for sure. What are you – a pony?"

"No, I'm a miniature horse, a small horse."

"Well, when are you going to grow up?"

"I'm as big as I'll ever get." Dreams of my youth came crashing back as I remembered my longing to be big like Thunder. I shook my mane and swished my tail.

"What do you do?" Dreamer asked with a snicker. "I mean, what good are you to humans?"

I dropped my head, feeling insecure and useless, feelings that I thought I'd put at bay long ago. "I don't know what good I am," I answered softly. "My first caregivers simply loved having me around, but things changed when they disappeared. I went from a wonderful place to a not-so-nice place to a horrible place, and now I'm here, but I've never figured out what use I am to humans."

Dreamer dislodged the flies from her face with a toss of her mane. "Well, I suppose you're cute enough, but you are very skinny, like many of us."

I peered around Dreamer's flanks and saw several other horses, and all were thin enough to have their ribs showing. I knew I looked the same.

"Why are all of us thin?" I asked. "I know that I wasn't fed for a very long time; why are you thin?"

"Just like you, I wasn't fed, and on top of that, I developed rainrot from not being able to get out of the weather."

"Rainrot?"

"Yeah. Sores developed all over my back, which had a fungus – really yucky and painful. I've been here for many months and am recovering nicely, but my hair still has white spots where my skin isn't completely healed." Dreamer pawed the dry earth with her hoof.

"What is this place anyway?"

"When I got here, I asked the same question. It's a rehabilitation farm, a place for wounded and thin and broken horses to get well. Once we're well enough, we'll go to new homes with human caregivers that will take proper care of us."

"I don't ever want to leave this place. It's pretty and safe. I like it here."

"Well, we'll all leave. Horses have come and gone since I arrived. Some were in better condition than others, but with all the wonderful care given here, they soon recovered and went with new caregivers."

I looked around at my surroundings – blue sky open above, trees and grass as far as my good eye could see, and a pond across the road from the pasture. No, I never wanted to leave this place.

"Well, you'll get to meet the other horses during the coming days," Dreamer whinnied as she turned around, "and each has a story to tell that will make you cry. I'm sure you have the same."

I watched Dreamer amble back to the other horses, where I could sense that she was telling them about me as curious glances were cast my way, but they never stopped munching the hay that was in the feeder before them. I was curious about them, for sure, but grazing was my primary interest, and it took all my energy to stay upright and graze at the same time. Occasionally, I heard snickers from the other horses, but I think their curiosity about me was quenched by the desire to eat continuously to make up for all the days food had been absent.

The sun warmed my back as flies buzzed around my head, and I found myself shaking my mane constantly to rid myself of those nasty creatures as I ate my way around my small enclosure.

Suddenly, I heard dogs barking, and I bolted and fell to the ground, terror coursing through my veins! Dogs! Why were dogs here, in this place that I thought was safe? Dogs had mauled me and torn my ear when I was helpless and flat out on the ground; the sound of their barking ignited fear that raced through me like lightning. I struggled to regain my footing quickly as I saw the dogs come out of the house with one of my caregivers. They were jumping and barking and running around her, but they paid absolutely no attention to me.

My caregiver made her way toward me, and I saw her open a gate and close it, containing the dogs, which started playing with each other and running around their large enclosure surrounding the house. My heart slowed its frantic pace as I leaned into the fence.

My caregiver opened my gate and came to me, stretched out her hand and gave me a large slice of apple. I smelled it before I could actually see it. I immediately consumed it as the fear melted away. These dogs were obviously not vicious like the ones that had attacked me. I'd known other dogs that were kind also, so these creatures meant me no harm, and I started to relax under the loving hand stroking my neck.

When I was led to my paddock for the night, I crashed into the fresh bed of straw and went soundly asleep. It had been a great day.

August 27, 2008 – Sassy is continuing to improve, enjoying time outside grazing and talking with the farm horses at the rehab farm. She amazes us daily with her zest to want to live and enjoy being a horse. Her eyesight in her right eye is obviously good enough to identify objects clearly (even a TB syringe from across the stall), and it is doing well. So we are still hopeful that her sight will remain in that eye. Round the clock care is being provided to administer eye meds every 2 hours. Her caregivers are tired, but enjoying this little one with so much personality.

August 28, 2007 – It's hard to believe how far Sassy has come in her recovery! The strength in her weakened legs has been getting slowly stronger over the past week. She's much like a human patient that's been ill for a long time or had surgery and on bed rest for an extended period. Like them, she's had to rebuild atrophied muscle and relearn muscle memory of how to use her legs. And her improvements are very noticeable every day. Just yesterday, grazing was a slow process for her as she relearned how to place her feet so she could reach the grass. In one day, she mastered that skill and can now graze with the best of them.

Another wonderful step in her recovery is that many of her blood values are returning to the normal range, although she is still very anemic (it takes several weeks to months to fully recover from anemia). Her right eye is also doing good with the "round-the-clock" meds. She is standing, walking, eating and being a horse most of the day, with a couple of naps lying down to "refuel." And although she can be wobbly when she gets tired, her improvements every day astound us.

Still, her journey to recovery is an uphill climb and we hold our breath that no setbacks occur to interfere with the inexplicable improvements Sassy has shown consistently during her battle. USERL is very grateful for the professional and compassionate care she received at NCSU Veterinary Hospital, as well as the support offered by so many of you. It is a great effort for one so little --- and Sassy is taking full advantage of the support offered to her.

Even though I spent a lot of time grazing and eating oats, the strength in my legs was slow to return. Often, I got frustrated when I couldn't stand up quickly, for my legs would collapse under me – I was getting heavier by the day – and I would get angry after several failed attempts to get on my feet. One of my caregivers frequently rubbed my legs and bent them and stretched them while I stood; I don't know why, but it seemed to help them feel better, if not stronger, too.

Walking was easy now, but what I really wanted to do was run, with the wind blowing through my mane and my tail streaming out behind me! Oh, to run again! Dreams of running through the fields with Thunder, Patches, Buttercup and Mother frequented my sleep as I struggled through the difficult time of recovery. I knew it wouldn't be easy. It had taken months for me to end up in my horrible condition, and to get back to being strong and healthy again would probably take as long, if not longer.

Remarkably, my eyesight was improving, something I never thought would happen. Things were much clearer, and on occasion, I could even see small objects and my caregivers as they worked in the distance. Upon my arrival, I'd decided that if my eyesight never improved, I would accept it. As long as I was safe, secure and well fed, having good eyesight paled in comparison.

August 30, 2007 - …. Sassy is doing very well, still improving every day. She will need more time to regain strength in her atrophied muscles. She has limited motion in her hind legs, which frustrates her at this time when she is trying to stand up. Sassy is getting physical therapy to improve range of motion in these legs, and it is improving little by little.
Her right eye is still improving as well! And her contentment with her current lot in life is evident…. Sassy is so eager to enjoy life that she wears herself out by afternoon and takes more frequent naps in the evenings (starting back up with her renewed energy at 3 am!) Caring for her closely resembles caring for a toddler!
Sassy is overcoming so many obstacles (many that no one can explain), so we will continue to let Sassy lead us through her recovery one day at a time and just be amazed with her 'sass'.

Mornings came quickly as I slept soundly from all my activities during the day. Often I'd whinny at my caregivers and stomp the paddock floor to get their attention if they were slow in letting me outside in the mornings. I would be so eager to get outside that I often tried to run, which surprised my caregivers, so they started putting a halter and leadline on me to keep me from going too fast. It felt fabulous to be able to move quickly after so much time spent lying down and sleeping.

It was still the hot season, and even though I loved being outdoors again, the heat was difficult to endure. My caregivers were wonderful though, and they were quick to see that, for some strange reason, I couldn't sweat like I used to. Instead of being put out to graze in the daytime, they started putting me out at night, after the sun disappeared, and it was so much more comfortable for me. During the days when it was hot, they fixed this contraption that sprayed a very fine mist of water into my stall, which cooled the air around me and cooled my back, making the hot days bearable. I often whinnied and nuzzled whoever was close by in order to show my gratitude for all the kind things that were done for me.

I felt better each passing day and knew that I had nothing to fear, that I would recover completely and be able to run again.

August 31, 2007 – Sassy continues to improve, getting stronger every day. She is now quite persistent when she wants to go out and graze, so a halter and leadline are now needed at times to keep her from going too fast! Her right eye is doing great and the infection in her left eye has been under control all week. Eye medication treatments were reduced to every 4 hours (yeah!) Thursday afternoon.
One problem Sassy is having is the heat. She cannot sweat right now (a common problem with weakened horses) as her body was so depleted of proper nutrition. So she now has a misting system in her stall to help keep her cool during the daytime heat, and she is often turned out for a 'midnight' graze instead.

One day, the hot air was replaced by cool weather, and I was actually able to go out and graze with the other horses. I explored the entire space, a large pasture, and met some of the other horses as they inspected me through the fence that separated us. Dreamer was right there, introducing me to some of the other horses.

Sweet and gentle Chelsea had problems with her teeth that her caregivers failed to address, and she couldn't eat because of it and became extremely thin. At the rehabilitation farm, she had some dental work done and could then eat like the rest of us. She was well on her way to recovery when I met her.

Cisco's legs were in horrible condition when he had arrived. Sores had festered for so long that they were horribly infected. The treatment was long and painful for him, and he was still recovering and for many months later as well.

Cinnamon was very thin, left in an enclosure with other horses, some of which died due to lack of feed. Cinnamon was gentle and kind and quiet, and all she wanted to do was eat all day long, and I couldn't blame her in the least.

Day after day, as I grazed, I learned of the horrible conditions that other horses had endured, but I didn't feel ready to tell my story just yet. Things were still too fresh in my mind, too painful to relive again, so I listened to the tragedies the others had endured.

Being small, horses of average size were huge compared to me, but when I met Diesel, the word HUGE wasn't adequate. Diesel was a draft horse, I learned, one that could pull a lot more weight than most horses as he was large and powerful, but poor Diesel was bony and had horrible sores all over his face, causing most of his hair to fall out. He looked frightful, actually, but his heart was gentle, and he found me most intriguing.

"So, you're Sassy, the small horse," he stated as Dreamer introduced him. "I've never seen a horse as small as you, that's for sure, and I must say that you look rather hilarious!"

I tried not to take offense. "Well, Diesel, I tried to get bigger, but no matter how much I ate – and that was when I had food to eat – I never got big. There was another horse where I used to live – Thunder was his name – and I admired him so much and longed to be big like him, but my mother explained that I was a miniature horse and that I'd never be the size of most horses." I reached up and stuck my muzzle through the fence. "I've come to accept that; it doesn't bother me that I'm small."

Diesel stood beside me and nudged me with his muzzle. "Welcome to our farm," he snorted. "I'm sure you've heard the stories of some of the horses here, but we haven't heard yours. Would you like to tell us?"

Dreamer shook her head. "Yes, please tell us, Sassy. It looks like you've had it worse than some of us, with your eyes being cloudy and your body so thin, your ear ripped and sores all over you, although they are healing quite nicely. Yes, please tell us your story."

The other horses within hearing range whinnied their agreement. "Yes, tell us your story, Sassy."

I looked around at the motley group, horses that had suffered as had I, and finally realized that the time to tell my story had come.

And so I did.

When I finished, all eyes were on me, and most of the grazing had ceased. All I could hear was the sound of swishing tails chasing away the flies.

"Indeed, you have had it worse, Sassy. We're glad you made it, and you'll make a wonderful companion for another horse when you leave this farm."

I sighed and shook my head. "Yes, life has been hard, and not just for me, but for all of you, too. Right now, I'm exhausted from talking and bringing up the past. I'd like to simply enjoy the day and my new friends."

I returned to grazing, as did the others. There wasn't any more talk that day about the suffering we had all endured.

Later that same day, as the clouds hung low in the sky, a young caregiver came and snapped a leadline to my halter and led me from the pasture. She brushed me and combed my mane and tail, and then she braided my mane. Her hands running through my mane felt wonderful, and I relished the lavish attention she was giving me. Afterward, she fed me carrots and apple slices. I think the other horses wished they could get some of the attention I was getting, but they never held the extra care against me.

September 1, 2007 – The cooler weather today was fantastic for Sassy. She was very active in her exploration of the farm, meeting the horses and grazing along the fence line with them. They were mesmerized by her, . . . and she was content to hang out with other equines. A young USERL volunteer played "My Little Pony" with her, and Sassy sported braids and pony tails all over. She loves attention and follows people around for scratches and treats.

Day by day, I got stronger and healthier. I could see that I was putting on weight, but sometimes things weren't quite right with me. I was given some sort of medicine that made me pass a lot of manure, which wasn't too pleasant. My caregivers constantly pried my mouth open and looked inside, rubbing fingers along my gums and talking a lot. I had no idea why they kept looking there; it's not like they ever found something and took it out.

On the day I dropped a lot of manure, I felt very tired and slept a lot. I guess I couldn't be active all the time quite yet. By the next day, I was feeling much better and noticed that I could get up by myself quite easily, which thrilled me. As usual, I insisted on going outside, but was kept in my stall with the mister going to keep me cool as the sun had returned to heat the day.

My eyes, surprisingly, were getting better, and not just one, but both of them. I could see with both eyes well enough that I could spot my caregivers with the eye medicines in their hands when they entered my stall. Trying to escape the medications for my eyes while in my stall is impossible; I always got caught.

I had noticed that my hooves were still in need of trimming. I'd had several trimmings already, each one a step in getting my hooves back to normal. Again, my caregivers were diligent in providing for my needs, and I was taken on my leadline outside my stall, held by a caregiver, and had my hooves trimmed by the same man who'd done them before. I did not make it easy for him. I kept kicking out my feet and trying to walk away, but he eventually managed to accomplish the task. I never did like having my hooves trimmed, but I suppose it's for my own good as it made walking much easier. Many of the other horses had their hooves trimmed, too, and I'm happy to report that some of them also gave the man a difficult time.

Grazing after the sun disappeared became the norm for quite some time. Only on cloudy, cool days was I allowed outside, which I loved because I could mingle with the other horses.

September 3, 2007 – Sassy has had an incredible weekend! She had a quiet day Saturday, probably due to her whirlwind activity on Friday as well as being dosed with dewormer (her gums were pale Saturday). But Sunday Sassy returned to her inquisitive self and is now more independent; can get up and down on her own, walks strongly and can get away faster when she sees the eye meds or thermometer in hand. Her eyes are doing wonderful, with sight remaining in her right eye. A young farrier, Frank Marques, came by to trim horses and worked on her hooves. Sassy put up quite a fight and will be a handful when she is fully recovered, but she now sports more normal looking hooves (and it has helped her mobility tremendously!). She's had four hoof trims since she arrived to slowly get her hooves trimmed back to normal. Her physical therapy to strengthen atrophied hind leg muscles has also made a big difference in her mobility. She can now flex her hocks and stifles almost normally.

She continues to "not sweat", so this is the main concern of this week as temperatures get hotter again. Luckily, her misting fan and cooling alcohol baths do the trick. It is unlikely she will return to sweating this year as it has taken a minimum of six months to replenish past rehab horses to where they could once again sweat.

Wonderful volunteers and 4-H teenagers gave the foster a much needed break over the weekend. Their giving of time and care was much appreciated! Sassy's remarkable recovery from such a guarded prognosis would not be possible without all the support for her. She's now out of immediate danger, but still has a long way to go for a full recovery. USERL thanks all that contribute for her.

Chapter Eleven

Life was pretty uneventful, but another change occurred one day. I was moved to a different stall that had a low wall on one side, and an older mare was in the other stall. Once we were left alone, I walked over and lifted my head so she could touch my muzzle.

"Ah, you are a little one," she softly neighed.

Those words, 'little one', brought a lump to my throat. Mother's name for me would forever be dear to my heart.

"My mother used to call me Little One, but my name is now Sassy," I replied as I smelled her scent. "What is your name?"

"Lizzie."

"What brought you here?"

"Oh, much the same thing as the other horses here – lack of feed and water. It's been a very strange year, very little rain and lots of heat, and the grass hasn't grown very much, so many of us here simply didn't have enough grass on which to graze. I'm starting to put on weight now."

"Me, too."

"Where is your mother?"

I dropped my head and looked away. "I don't know. We were together until those horrible humans took me away, and I never saw her after that. They were the ones who were supposed to care for me but didn't, and I almost fell into the long sleep that never ends."

"Yes, I heard your story when you told it. I was behind the others as they listened. It is quite a tragic story."

"No more tragic, I guess, than some of the others. I'll never understand why humans don't care for the animals in their charge, but these humans here and at the other place I was before I came here, they are wonderful. I'm feeling so much better, but I know I still have a long way to go."

"Well, just keep eating and enjoying yourself, and you'll be well before you know it. I'm happy to have you next to me, Sassy. We will become good friends."

Life with Lizzie next door was good. When she wasn't out to pasture, she was in her stall next to me, and I appreciated her gentle company. She enjoyed the benefit of my cooling mist as much as I did!

My days were still filled with eye medications, therapy for my legs, and lots of eating and grazing. Remarkably, I could trot for short spurts, which thrilled me tremendously! I finally started feeling like the horse I used to be, and I looked forward to the day when I would finally be able to run straight out, hooves flying, and clods of dirt sailing through the air behind me.

September 9, 2007 – Sassy is still recovering great! After a follow-up with our veterinarian on Thursday, Sassy's eye meds have been changed somewhat since they are doing so well. She still requires eye meds every 4 to 6 hours to ensure her right eye continues to have sight.
A double stall was partitioned with a low wall so that Sassy can have socialization with an older, gentle mare during her rehab. She is enjoying the companionship.
Sassy is slowly gaining weight, and with it strength. She now does a half trot when she wants to get somewhere in a hurry. The flexibility in her legs continues to improve with physical therapy.

Now that I was feeling better, I guess you could say that I had a little attitude. When someone didn't let me out to graze or feed me my oats on time, I'd whinny and whinny and stomp around – well, as much stomping as a miniature horse could do – until my demands were met. My caregivers became quite adept at understanding me.

Exploring the farm became one of my favorite pastimes. I'd wander around, poke my head into or under things, and check out everything within my reach. Occasionally, I got to wander down to the pond and found a few frogs to chase, but just like when I was young, they always heard me coming and jumped into the water. It's impossible to get them when that happens.

Eating is still the main activity of my days. Whether it is grass, oats, apples and treats, it doesn't matter. All of the horses ate constantly, so I wasn't any different, but when my caregiver poured fresh feed in my bucket, I heard it and went running back to my stall, eager to dig in. My caregiver laughed when I showed up and poured a bit more feed into my bucket as I chomped away.

One day, as I was out exploring, there was a loud bang, and I trotted as fast as I could back to my stall. Lizzie was out grazing, and she didn't run back, but whatever the noise was scared me, so I felt safer in my stall. I was amazed at how fast I'd moved when I was scared. I guess my recovery was progressing quite nicely.

September 11, 2007 – Sassy continues to improve daily. She is quite mobile and demanding about where she wants to go – which is usually graze or eat. She came back into the barn to eat her feed (she heard the foster pouring it in her bucket). Her personality is delightful and she's enjoying exploring the farm. She got startled by a loud noise yesterday and came trotting quickly into the barn, navigating around muck buckets and shaving bags to get back to her stall. So her muscle strength is improving great and her eye sight in her right eye continues to remain good as well.

Oddly, the other horses saw me as a leader, which I found completely strange. They allowed me to boss them around, let me eat first, and followed me wherever I went in the pasture. They actually argued over who was going to stand next to me and use their tail to keep the flies from my eyes. Because my eyesight was still poor in my right eye and practically nonexistent in my left eye, they were attentive to where I went and how I got there. Apparently my eyes were quite the topic of conversation, I discovered.

"Sassy can't see much," I heard Diesel say to Dreamer as I stood close by. "Her eyes have a strange color, not like the rest of ours."

"I know," agreed Dreamer. "They're cloudy and gray, but one is brighter than the other."

"What happened to your eyes?" Diesel asked.

"I think it was the flies that bit me all the time when I was alone," I said. "They were nasty, biting constantly, and my eyes itched and swelled. I remember that I could hardly see when I collapsed."

"Can you see now?"

"Some out of one eye, and now I'm starting to see light out of the other. For a while, I thought I'd never see well again, but now I'm hoping that I will. The humans here take such good care of me, and even though I try to get away when I see them coming with my eye medicine, I really appreciate how it's helping me to see again."

Dreamer nudged me. "Well, you let us take care of you until you can see well again."

And they all did. Never did I go anywhere without one of the other horses walking beside me.

Visitors were frequent at the farm, and for some odd reason, I got lots of attention from the visitors. I loved it! Endless treats and chin and ear scratches. Whenever I saw a strange car come down the drive, I'd hurry over to the fence, hoping for a little extra attention, and I always got it. Mind you, I got plenty, especially from Tiffanygirl, who brushed and braided my mane constantly, but treats from strangers were always nice.

Once I had eaten the treat, I'd trot around, break into a short run, and even kick up my heels to show off my newfound strength in my legs! I was feeling grand!

September 14, 2007 – Sassy is living up to her name and ruling the farm. She's active – trotting, cantering, and bucking as she enjoys her new lease on life. She continues to capture the hearts of all who visit her, showing her zest for life with extensive explorations of the farm and exuberant antics.
Her eyes continue to do well and the eye medications will continue for quite some time to ensure her sight remains.
Thanks again to all who have supported this little gal and to those who will be. Sassy has embraced this second chance and run with it!

My strength continued to grow with each passing day, and soon I was trotting and galloping through the fields. The other horses continually cheered me on, knowing what I had endured and how much I loved life. My eyesight also improved, and seeing became less of a problem. Soon, I was able to detect small objects and things in the distance, like Dreamer and Cisco and the other horses at the far end of the pasture.

My ribs didn't stick out like they used to; my mane flowed in the breeze when I ran; my tail streamed out behind me, and I was quite proud of myself! Oftentimes, I'd run until I tired myself out, and visitors, which were still frequent, would watch from the fence as I ran like lightning. Thoughts of Thunder and how he'd run so fast often came to mind, and even though I knew I wasn't running nearly as fast as he'd run, I truly felt like I was flying! Oh, it felt so good to have strong legs! My days of lying down for hours on end were finally over.

My caregivers and Tiffanygirl, and often humans I didn't know at all, frequently brushed me, and I never complained. It felt wonderful to be brushed, especially after not being groomed for a very long time. However, when a volunteer came at me with a bucket of water, the hose, and everything else used to bathe me, I tried to get away, but couldn't. They had secured me before the items came into my view, which I didn't think was in the least bit fair!

Now, not having been bathed for such a long time, I'd forgotten what it was like, and I didn't particularly enjoy the process of being hosed down, soaped up, scrubbed, and hosed again. Pulling on my lead in an effort to get away was useless, but that didn't mean that I didn't try. My volunteer was patient with me, and I eventually settled down, especially when the hosing was over and the process of brushing me down began.

Once I was done, I was released, and I broke away and ran as fast as I could. Dreamer laughed at me as I kicked up my heels.

"Didn't like your bath, hey?"

I pulled to a quick stop not far from her. "Well, I can't say that I enjoyed it, but I definitely like the result. I feel so much better."

"And you look better, too," snorted Charlotte. "I've had too many baths to count; this rain rot requires a lot of treatment and a lot of bathing."

I shook my head in an effort to dry my mane. "Well, you look better all the time, Charlotte. Your coat is much shinier than when I arrived."

"True, true. And you look quite nice now that your ribs don't stick out any longer. You're quite a good looking horse, if I may say so, even if you are tiny."

"Now, now," Dreamer interrupted, "all of us look a lot better than when we arrived, and once we completely recover, we'll be handsome horses again. We were all beautiful animals at one time, and we will be once more."

The rest of the day I spent grazing with the big horses, and I realized how happy I was and how very lucky to have been found in time.

September 22, 2007 – Sassy continues to get stronger and is thriving at this time. She is simply being a horse and enjoying it thoroughly! Her eyes are doing great, and she has no other immediate problems at this time other than to gain to a healthy weight.
A volunteer gave Sassy her first real bath today. Sassy wasn't sure she liked it, but her coat has finally shed the dead hair almost completely out.

    The hot weather slowly dissipated as the days became shorter, which was wonderful as I could go out and graze with the other horses during the day, no matter if the sun was shining. I ate constantly, and I think the other horses thought I was not a horse, but a pig!

    In the meantime, Lizzie became my constant companion. She was quiet and patient and put up with my silliness all the time. She became more like a mother to me than a friend, and she made sure that the new horses on the farm never made fun of me for being small and never took advantage of me or hurt me in any way. We often grazed side-by-side, head to rear, swishing each other's tails to assist in deflecting flies from each other's faces. I was comfortable with Lizzie, and she with me.

    The one eye that had given me so much trouble was, surprisingly, getting much better, and I thought that maybe I shouldn't put up such a fuss about the eye medications. I could actually see out of that eye, and the other one had good vision. These changes were so slow and small that I often didn't realize something had changed until several days had passed, and then it would suddenly dawn on me that I could see better.

The weather was hot one day and nice the next, so my grazing times were constantly changing. Sometimes I'd be let out in the early morning, but other times, I was kept in my stall with my wonderful mister and not let out until the sun was going away for the night. I never knew from day to day what time I was going to be let out to graze. The land was still dry from lack of rain, but when rain occasionally did fall, it revived the grass overnight, but then the sun would dry things out again. The other horses were constantly talking about the dry land and wondered when the rains would return on a regular basis.

October 10, 2007 – Sassy is doing very well. Her weight gain is steady ….. she is energetic and playful. Her eyes are doing great, with the scarring on her left eye shrinking enough for her to have very slight vision in it! Her right eye has close to full vision. So Sassy has once again overcome what could have been a heartbreaking ending (blindness). No one could have predicted this outcome, so we are very thankful to all that helped with the multiple eye meds for so many weeks. She continues to receive one eye medicine to prevent a reoccurrence of bacterial and/or fungal infections in the eyes.

Sassy and her companion graze quietly together. Due to the return of hot weather, she has only been able to go outside in the early evening or nighttime hours. Now that cool weather is returning, she can go out more without worry of overheating.

Just as the leaves were donning the slightest hint of color before falling to the ground, I was confined and clipped – not just brushed, but clipped! I know I shouldn't complain, but sometimes there's just no getting around it. Now that I was feeling so much better, I really didn't like standing still for all that beauty stuff, even though I remembered how gorgeous Mother looked after a bath and brushing and hoof trimming. Naturally, I fussed and gave my opinion loudly and clearly, but after realizing that all the primping felt good, I stood still and enjoyed it. Lizzie laughed at me, but I didn't care. When I saw all the hair that ended up on the ground, I wondered if I was bald, but upon further examination, I discovered that there was plenty of hair remaining, and despite my initial complaining, I did look rather fine, if I must say so myself. Lizzie agreed.

"My, my, Sassy, you're quite the little horse now, all spiffed up like that! I never knew you could look so good!"

I swished my tail proudly. "Thanks, Lizzie! I feel really good, too. Just wish I didn't have to go through all this fuss to look as good as I feel!"

Even though the leaves were starting their changing process, the temperatures were still quite warm, and my coat had become rather thick, which made me hot, and that wasn't a good thing since I still couldn't sweat, which was the main reason for the clipping. My mister was still used quite frequently in my paddock.

October 18, 2007 – Sassy continues to blossom and capture the hearts of all who meet her. Today she was body clipped by a

USERL volunteer, Barbara Cohen. The continuing warm temperatures were a concern as she began growing her winter coat. Sassy did very well for her clipping, standing still most of the time. Thank you, Barbara, for volunteering to do this for Sassy!

I loved every day! As soon as I was let out of my paddock, I'd take off running all over the farm. Often I was allowed to go where I wanted, no fences in my way, gates open and inviting. I loved getting my feet wet on the edge of the pond and often would chase those hoppy frogs that lived there. I'd gallop through the fields with the cheers of the other horses ringing in my ears. You see, running like the wind was finally possible, and the other horses understood what a great thing it was to be able to run since many of them had been unable to do so themselves. Yes, I'd run like the wind, fast as my legs would go, mane flying in the breeze and my tail trailing behind me! What a wonderful feeling!

My eyesight was almost back to normal. Some blurred vision still remained, but I was certainly not complaining. There was nothing that I couldn't do now that I could see again.

My clipped coat allowed me to go outside most days as I didn't get overheated easily. I could feel the breeze lifting the hairs on my back, and it was like the touch of the Creator stroking me, letting me know that he cared.

I think it was around that time that I began to accept that I'd never see Mother again. Even though this made me sad, I shook away my sadness and embraced my life as it was. I was safe and loved, fed and sheltered, even pampered, and I believed in my heart that Mother had found the same in her life. That was the only way I could avoid getting depressed at her absence.

As the days passed, we were blessed with rain – not much, but some, and more frequently. The fields starting greening up as the rains fell and washed the dust from the trees and bushes. We welcomed any rain.

October 19, 2007 – Sassy zips around the farm feeling 'cooler' with her new clipped haircoat. Her energy is great and her eyes are doing wonderful!

October 21, 2007 – Sassy is filling out nicely with fat and muscle returning where it should be. Her diet is simple (hay and feed) and she is gaining weight easily. Exercise has been important to rebuild the atrophied muscles from lack of use and malnutrition. Her heart is now stronger and her mobility is completely normal! Of course, it helped that Sassy was so small. An average size horse would have been almost impossible to support through this rehabilitation. Sassy is definitely a very lucky horse to have had all who have been involved with her rescue: Tori – Harnett County's appointed Cruelty Investigator; Harnett County Animal Control, NCSU College of Veterinary Medicine, Neuse River Veterinary Hospital and all the USERL volunteers that have given selflessly to care for her throughout her rehabilitation. Sassy and USERL thank you for all you have done and are doing for her!

The trees on the trees turned those brilliant colors that I love to see, and the tree shadows stretched out long across the fields. Some of the other horses mended enough to be adopted and were taken away to new homes. Others, such as Dreamer and Charlotte, continued to mend at the farm while still a few others arrived with their own stories of neglect and horror.

Now that the temperatures were cooling down in the day, I wasn't restricted in my outdoor activity. However, some days were still very warm, and my mister had to be turned on again to keep me cool. Other days were chilly, and I was covered with a blanket when I went outside. It must have been made just for me because it fit wonderfully.

As time passed, the horror of my ordeal began to fade from my memory. My sleep was peaceful. I no longer feared the dogs that lived on the farm with me. Lizzie and I pretty much hung out together, grazing and dozing in the warm sun on those days when the sun was so gentle that it put you to sleep.

My body continued to gain strength and weight. My legs were completely recovered and could take me anywhere I wanted at any speed I desired. My tail, now full and golden, hung down to the ground. My eyesight was almost completely recovered. My caregivers were constantly chattering about my recovery and praising me for how well I'd done when really, it wasn't me at all, but all of them. Those were true caregivers, not like the ones who had me before I almost went to sleep forever. Those caregivers truly cared for the horses – and dogs, chickens, donkeys, goats, and other critters I can't name – in their care.

Without them, I'd never have been able to recover from my ordeal.

November 21, 2007 – A wonderful lady donated 2 miniature blankets for Sassy. She had grown a thick winter coat in September, which was clipped to keep her cool due to her inability to sweat and cool off. But now the weather is changing every week (sometimes warm, sometimes cold), so Sassy will certainly be able to make use of her blanket on those chilly days.

November 23, 2007 – Sassy continues to do well, gaining weight very easily. So easily, in fact, that she's now on very little feed/hay. Her muscle tone is improving with all the exercise she's getting, and her eyes continue to amaze everyone. With almost full sight in her right eye, and her left eye with some sight, Sassy's future is bright! As long as her left eye continues to do so well, the anticipated surgery to remove it has been cancelled.

Chapter Twelve

As the leaves fell and the weather turned cold, the rains came. Glorious, wonderful rain! The ground turned muddy under my hooves, water dripped from the trees, and the pond was freshened by the rains. Because it was the cold season, the grass was no longer green, but hay was plentiful, and we braved the muddy fields daily to eat from the feeders.

As the frost covered the earth during the cold nights, I'd stand in my warm stall next to Lizzie's and savor all my blessings. Gone was my mister; instead, I often wore my warm blankets, as did the other horses when it was cold and frosty. I still had frequent visitors and treats, chin scratches, and ear scratches. The thought that I could possibly leave this wonderful place never occurred to me until Lizzie mentioned it.

"Well, Sassy, now that you're fully recovered, are you ready to go to a new home?"

I jerked my head up in surprise, my mouth full of oats. I swallowed hard and blinked. "I really hadn't thought about it, Lizzie. I like it here. I don't want to leave."

Lizzie swished her tail. "Well, all of us go to new homes when we're well; I hope to do the same some day."

"But I want to stay here," I whinnied. Fear crept into my heart. As the day progressed, my worries didn't stop. I wished that Lizzie simply hadn't raised the subject of being adopted.

A few days later, I was taken from my stall, haltered, and led into a trailer. I threw my head up and neighed when I saw the trailer; indeed, I was going to leave this wonderful place! I didn't want to go! But in gratefulness to those who had given me such good care, I loaded into the trailer without trouble. Surely they'd make sure that I went to a good place!

The trailer swayed and lurched, eventually stopping. As the ramp was lowered, I heard vaguely familiar voices, and I turned my head in surprise. It was the caregiver who had first cared for me when I was in such horrible condition, the one who stayed with me and fed me mush every few hours!

When I was untethered, I hurried down the ramp and whinnied a glad greeting. Soon, loving arms encircled my neck, and my favorite caregiver of all time knelt beside me and scratched my ears. It was wonderful! I was so glad to see her, and I wondered if she was going to take me to stay with her forever. That would be the absolute best thing – next to staying at the rescue farm.

I was allowed to run through an enclosure as the caregivers watched and laughed as I kicked up my heels.

Everyone who was standing along the fence held little boxes that they pointed at me and then looked at, but I have no idea what they were. The sun was shining, and my thick winter coat kept the cold at bay. Even though I'd spent many days at this place, I couldn't remember arriving, and I really didn't want to remember. I wanted to forget everything that had caused me pain and suffering.

After some time, I was again put in the trailer, and my caregiver gave me one last affectionate scratch. After a brief ride, I was back at the farm. Lizzie welcomed me with questioning eyes.

"I thought you'd gone to a new home," she said.

"That's where I thought I was going, but I was taken to visit the wonderful caregiver who had first treated me when I was rescued. It was so good to see her again! And she was happy to see me, too. I'll bet she could hardly believe her eyes. The last time she'd seen me, I couldn't even get up on my legs."

"And now you're back here."

"Yes, Lizzie, and I hope I stay, but if I go somewhere else, I know that I'll go to humans who will take proper care of me. I'm okay with that now."

But I never did go anywhere else. I stayed on the farm. Horses came and horses went, but I stayed, and I began to understand that it was my new home. My days were filled with love and fun. I made it a point to get to know every horse that came, to find out their stories, and to let them know that there are good, kind humans in the world and that they'll be well again and have a wonderful home.

December 12, 2007 – So many have been following the inspiring story of Sassy, a miniature mare who was seized in Harnett County on August 15th of this year. The owners, Alex Smith and Tiffany Conlen, pled guilty to 1 count misdemeanor animal cruelty, received a suspended 12-month sentence and can no longer own horses.
Sassy was awarded to Harnett County, who has given permanent custody of the little mare to USERL. Many thanks to Harnett County for their diligent work on this case.
And the best news is, she's now completely healthy. Her right eye has only a very small scar and her left eye has some sight. An incredible recovery for a remarkable little mare!

Sassy returned to the NCSU College of Veterinary Medicine to surprise everyone with Christmas cheer, and much deserved Thank You's!

Dr. Keller of NCSU College of Veterinary Medicine, who tirelessly cared for Sassy during her stay at the hospital, was thrilled to see Sassy and her new-found health. Sassy gave her thanks to Dr. Keller and others at the hospital by posing for photos and being her adorable self. Many thanks to Dr. Keller, Dr. Brauhaus, the talented veterinary technicians, and the Opthamology and Pharmacy departments for their excellent care and support of this little mare. Sassy is on to her new life and has all of you to thank for it!

The cold season that was upon us brought much-needed rains, rains that replenished the earth and filled the creeks, ponds, and streams. The air was fresh and clean as the sun started its climb and warmed the earth during the passing weeks. It was as if all of nature exploded with growth encouraged by the rains, and it was definitely a wonderful sight to see. As the days warmed, the pastures sprang to life with green, succulent grasses, and I was again reminded of what a pleasure it was to eat fresh green grass! When the dew was still on the grass early in the morning, it made the grass moist, and that was my favorite time to graze.

Lizzie no longer kept me company on a continual basis. My thoughts were often to the day when she'd be well enough to be adopted by new caregivers, and I tried to prepare myself for that time by spending a lot of my time with the others. Eventually, Lizzie found a loving family, and she was given the opportunity to say goodbye before she was taken away.

"Well, Sassy, I guess this is where our paths part," she softly neighed as she muzzled me. "I have thoroughly enjoyed getting to know you. I might never get to meet another miniature horse, you know, so this experience has been one I'll remember forever."

"I hope you have a wonderful life, Lizzie. You're a wonderful horse, and quite gorgeous now. I'm sure your new caregivers will take good care of you."

"I trust that, too, Sassy."

"I'm going to miss you."

"And I'll miss you, but you have the other horses to keep you company."

"I hope you will be with other horses in your new home."

"Surely I'll be," Lizzie whinnied as she nudged my back. "Remember, we are herd animals, and these wonderful caregivers understand our needs. I know I'll meet other horses at my new home."

Lizzie's new caregivers arrived shortly, and I watched with a mixture of sadness and gladness as she was loaded into her the trailer. Her rump was the last thing I saw as the trailer bounced down the gravel road to the paved road beyond the gates.

And so life on the farm passed. My days were filled with good things, good feed, loving hands, and a sense of peace at being in such a wonderful place. Every time a new rescued horse arrived on the farm, I was the center of attention because never, not once, had any of the horses seen a miniature horse such as myself! I found that utterly strange, but I understood their inquisitive spirits.

However, that all changed the day Tank arrived! I was startled to see another horse my size! For the first time since I'd left Mother, I was able to look another horse in the eye without straining my neck to do so.

Tank was put in my outside pen with me, and I immediately trotted over, doing my best not to laugh. He was the fattest horse, big or small, that I'd ever seen! He could hardly walk, he was so fat! However, my laughter was quickly suppressed when I noticed his hooves, and that's when I realized why he was at the farm.

"Well, hello," I softly neighed as I reached him. "I'm so glad to see another miniature horse. Welcome to our farm."

Tank looked at me with sadness and pain in his eyes. "What's your name?"

"I'm called Sassy. My mother used to call me Little One, but I haven't seen her since before I was rescued. What's your name?"

"They call me Tank."

"Glad to meet you, Tank. I think we're going to be good friends."

"How long have you been here?"

"Since the last hot season. I live here now." I nudged Tank's back with my muzzle. "What happened to your hooves, Tank?"

"They haven't been trimmed for a very long time, and it's very painful for me to stand, much less run or walk."

I glanced down at his hooves, and they indeed were in terrible shape. "Don't worry, Tank. You'll have your hooves trimmed while you are here. The caregiver who does that for us comes all the time, and most of the horses here don't put up too much of a fuss when being trimmed, but I have seen a horse or two kick the caregiver, which I think is totally inappropriate." I wasn't about to admit that I had done the same!

"Well, I won't kick, that's for sure. I can't wait to get them trimmed so I can walk properly."

And so began our relationship. Tank had to have his hooves trimmed several times before he was able to stand and walk properly, and his feed was reduced so he could lose some weight, too. Of all the neglected horses I'd met since I was rescued, Tank was the only one who had the problem of being overweight. I never did figure out how a neglected horse could be overweight, but Tank was!

As Tank recovered, we were put out to pasture together, and soon we were inseparable. It was almost like being with Mother again. Having another miniature horse was fabulous, and I hoped that Tank would be able to stay with me forever.

As luck would have it, Tank recovered fully and stayed with me on the farm. I think our caregivers saw how much we liked each other's company, being the only two miniature horses around, and decided to keep us together.

Our days were spent running through the pastures, chasing frogs down by the pond, and talking to the other rescued horses about their mistreatment and neglect.

And that brings me to the present. Tank and I are still happily living together on the farm, frolicking and chasing each other as if we were young colts again. We often talk long into the night as we look at the skies overhead and wonder about the strange ways of humans, how some can be so cruel and uncaring while others can be so kind and loving. Horses, and all other animals in the care of humans, are totally dependent on them for their needs, and if the caregivers fail in their jobs, we are the ones who suffer.

I often remember back to the small humans who hit me and laughed at me. Their parents were responsible for their care, and I never once saw one of their parents hit them or forget to give them something to drink when the sun was shining brightly down on them. I never saw their parents forget to feed them or leave them in the sun, but those same humans forgot to feed, water, and shelter me. Apparently they thought that I didn't have feelings, but I do.

As Tank and I live out our lives in our wonderful home, enjoying the company of many other horses, good feed, fresh water, shelter and lots of space to run free, we wonder at the horses who will be coming onto our farm, the ones that are now being neglected and abused. Thankfully, I was found by someone who cared enough to take me out of my horrible situation, and not a moment too soon.

The stories I hear from the other horses break my heart. Not all of the horses are rescued in time. Brandy was taken from a farm where three of the horses in her herd died before she was rescued. She was bone thin when she arrived and had sores on her legs. She told me that her caregivers didn't even remove the bodies of her dead friends from the field, but simply left them there to rot and stink, and she had a horrible time forgetting such a sight.

It's sad that such a thing happens to horses and other animals, but we hope someday that there will be no need for rescue farms and that all human caregivers will provide for the animals in their care. All of the horses on the farm are grateful for the wonderful care that we've been given.

I don't know if any of the other horses will ever share their stories with you, but I hope my story has brought to light the plight of many horses and that, if you are a caregiver of a horse, you will do your utmost to see that the horses in your charge are provided for properly. I can assure you that a horse provided for properly will give you his heart and do your bidding without question.

Well, I have to go. Another horse just arrived, and I need to find out what happened to him and let him know that this farm is a safe and wonderful place where he'll be able to recover and return to the magnificent animal he was when times were kinder, gentler, and more loving.

A note from the Author, Barbara N. Stewart: I've been a horse lover all of my life, although I've never had the privilege of owning such a magnificent animal. I've had to keep my animal ownership to cats, dogs, gerbils, hamsters, and the like! However, I still hope to be able to own a horse, even if it's after I retire.

I came into contact with USERL in the Research Triangle Park area of North Carolina while recovering from back surgery. I began to work with other volunteers at the local rescue farms on weekends to give the fosters a break from the constant work. This involvement grew into the desire to write Sassy's story in order to raise awareness of horse neglect, while also raising funds for the horses. Sassy's rescue and rehabilitation are true in every detail. The fact that she survived is a miracle in itself, but the fact that her eyesight recovered is a double miracle!

North Carolina, indeed much of the southeast, experienced an exceptional drought in 2007, which caused the number of rescued horses to double due to people being unable to feed their animals. The cost of hay spiked dramatically, thus adding further burdens on those who were struggling to feed livestock of all kinds. Sassy was one of the animals that suffered through that extremely dry spring and summer. Winter brought the return of adequate rains, but it took months to replenish the water supplies in the reservoirs, lakes, and ponds.

Writing this book has been a time-consuming, but highly enjoyable, task for me, and it is my prayer that the sale of this book will generate much-needed funds for horses, not only in the Triangle region, but in all of the United States. Horses are neglected for many reasons, but none of them are excusable. There is always a place for a horse to be brought if the owner is unable to care for it any longer – USERL is one of those places.

Please pass this book along or, better yet, purchase another copy and give it as a gift. A large portion of the purchase price of every book is donated for the care of horses, and the funds are always needed.

Acknowledgements

I would like to thank USERL for its tireless efforts in rescuing and rehabilitating abused and neglected horses. Without their efforts, Sassy and hundreds of other horses would not be alive today.

I would like to thank Jennifer Malpass, who posted detailed accounts of Sassy's arduous recovery on www.userltriangle.org, as well as photos that exposed her horrible condition at the time of her rescue and her eventual return to health. Jennifer has fostered many horses during the years and has even adopted some that particularly touched her heart.

I would like to thank all of the volunteers that made Sassy's recovery possible, as well as all of the medical staff at North Carolina State University College of Veterinary Medicine. Sassy is just one of many horses that they have brought back from the brink of death.

I would like to thank my husband, Bob, for putting up with my long hours at the computer, for his input, and for his assistance with the final product. He helped make this job enjoyable.

I would like to thank Kathy Horky and her work in organizing the Barn Moms, as well as all who volunteer for the Barn Mom workdays. You're a great group of people who do a great job. I learn a lot about horses when I'm able to be around you!

Finally, I would like to thank Sassy for having the fortitude and determination to survive.

Barbara N. Stewart

ABOUT THE AUTHOR: Barbara Stewart has been an avid reader and writer all of her life. She and her husband, Bob, live in North Carolina and enjoy spending time in their gardens, both vegetable and flower, entertaining, hiking, and biking, as well as time with their children and six grandchildren, all of whom live close by. When not working at her professional job, Barbara spends much of her time at her computer, working on other stories that beg to be told.

****

A CAT'S TALE – by Barbara Stewart, available for purchase at www.createspace.com/3369283
"You'll do well to stay away from the road when you're outside......the world is full of hazards for cats," warned Mr. Hissy.

Buddy, a black Maine Coon cat, gives an account of his life, which includes a near-death experience, among other things, in this unusual story. In his tale, only the cats talk, and Buddy tries to figure out the comings and goings of humans and other animals. As a kitten, Buddy's first encounter with another cat is with Mr. Hissy, an ornery, old cat belonging to his new human caretakers. Laugh along when Buddy discovers that parts of his body are missing after going to the vet and when he tells of his multiple hunting escapades. Follow Buddy through his adventures with his sister, Sissy, their arduous move from North to South, and the antics of his caregivers as he shares life's experiences from a feline point of view.

Made in the USA
Charleston, SC
08 December 2009